El Sabor De Mi Cocina
(The Flavor of My Kitchen)
By Connie G. Palacios
Copyright 2020

Hope Kelley Book Publishing
HopeKelleyBookPublishing.com
publish@HopeKelley.com
800.806.6240

Printed in the United States of America

All rights reserved solely by the author. The author guarantees all contents are original and do not infringe upon the legal rights of any other person nor work. No part of this book may be reproduced in any form without the written permission of the author.

El Sabor De Mi Cocina

El Sabor De Mi Cocina

EL SABOR DE MI COCINA

(The Flavor Of My Kitchen)

By

Connie G. Palacios

El Sabor De Mi Cocina

El Sabor De Mi Cocina

COOKBOOK SECTIONS

Contents	P. 7
Dedication	P. 9
Foreword	P. 11
About the Author	P. 13
Prologue	P. 15
Main Dishes	P. 17
Breads, Pastas, and Casseroles	P. 107
Pies, Cakes, and Cookies	P. 145
Beverages, Fudges, Candies, Salads, & More	P. 205

El Sabor De Mi Cocina

El Sabor De Mi Cocina

Dedication

First and foremost, I thank God and our Blessed Mother – Our Lady of Guadalupe/Fatima, for giving me strength and FAITH on all my endeavors.

*To my most valued inspirations, and In Loving Memory, I dedicate this cookbook. My grandmother, Consuelo D. Perez+, who loved collecting recipes and encouraged me to write. My father, Servando Guerrero, Sr+, who was always proud at everything and anything his children conquered. My aunt Maria Inez Colunga+, who was always my head cheerleader. My mother, Esmeralda R. Gutierrez, my husband, Manuel Palacios and my cousin, Carolina Y. Rocha - Parkman,
for being my #1 supporters.*

Furthermore, to the ones who always have my back 100%, my brothers, Servando Guerrero, Jr, Rene Guerrero, Sr, Juan F. Guerrero, Sr. My sister, Erika I. Cavazos, their families and all my nieces and nephews. The best gift they have ever given me.

~Connie G. Palacios~

Matthew 19:2

El Sabor De Mi Cocina

Special Thanks

With great honor and gratitude, I give a huge Thank You, to these special people in my life, for they contributed to bring life to this; my first book.

Servando Guerrero, Jr - Brother

Mr. & Mrs. Rene Guerrero, Sr - Brother

(Guerrero Express Trucking)

Mr. & Mrs. Juan F Guerrero, Sr - Brother

(J. Guerrero & Sons Trucking)

Carlos Perez, III - Cousin

I love you all more than you can imagine.

El Sabor De Mi Cocina

FOREWORD

Connie and I have known each other for 8 years now. We became amazingly fast friends. She is always cooking and brings some of her favorite dishes to work. I am from Iowa and she lived in Michigan for several years, so we have a lot in common. As far as food taste and family rituals. You will love all her recipes in this cookbook. I wish you the best of luck, my dear friend, with this- your first book.   ~Jean Ann Villarreal, Freer, TX.

Connie has been a friend of mine for many years. We worked together for some of them. She has fought several personal battles and conquered them all. I hope her cookbook is a huge success, as she deserves it. Best of luck from one dear friend to another.
~ Debera Hitchcock, Rothbury, Michigan

If it is one thing anyone knows about me is that I am a lover of all thing's food. From the first time I met Connie, I knew she was going to be an inspiration. The connection was captivating. The feeling was that I had known her for a lifetime. She embodies a multitude of qualities, one of which is charisma, and most importantly, genuineness. El Sabor de Mi Cocina, is a mouthwatering collection of simple yet scrumptious recipes that will surely rotate through your kitchen on a regular basis. With a happy and content heart,
~ Irisbel "Bell" Saenz - Freer, TX

Neighbors look out for one another and share with each other. The best sharing though, is the sharing of authentic homemade meals that are made with love.
~ Ed and Ruby Trevino - Hebbronville, TX

El Sabor De Mi Cocina

ABOUT THE AUTHOR

Connie Guerrero Palacios is a South Texas native who resides in Hebbronville, Texas. Raised by her maternal grandparents in a neighboring town, Bruni, Tx, she spent quality time learning and appreciating, family recipes that had, and continue to this day to bring so much joy to the people sharing these authentic home-cooked meals. Over the years, her immediate family expanded from being the eldest of five (three brothers; Servando Jr, Rene, Juan and one sister, Erika) to gaining two half siblings (one brother, Roberto and sister, Lissa) and three stepbrothers; Lionel, Domingo & Joe. Keeping family values and recipes close, her long standing dream, was to publish a cookbook full of family pride, with intentions of sharing joy and love with other families.

This cookbook has been a long dream of Connie's. Originating from a geographical area influenced by Mexican traditions and a splash of her family touch. Young Connie often wondered how she could share such great recipes filled with love to the masses. As she grew older and stepped into the role of cook, she recognized the happiness many reveled in, with each bite. This only strengthened her lifelong dream in organizing these family recipes into a cookbook. She can only hope you, as the reader, will experience the great delight and love she shares in this collective book of her family treasures, as it holds a great wealth of sentimental value. She is a firm believer in her favorite scripture that says, "With man this is impossible, but with God all things are possible." - Matthew 19:26.

Connie and her husband, Manuel Palacios, have walked side by side for twenty-one years. Currently, they care of two blue heeler dogs, one chihuahua, and a horse named Flicka. She has dedicated herself to the United States Postal Service for thirteen years, commuting eighty miles daily to work in Freer, Texas. In her downtime, she enjoys cooking, writing, fishing, reading, knitting, and crocheting. But the most valuable piece of her time is with her family.

Connie has experienced many challenges in her life; however, she fully recognizes each trial has led her to where she is now: stronger, wiser, and ever so grateful. Connie says life is a daily challenge that allows us to grow as we go. You never know what great things may arise from one day to the next. One must keep the Faith, then share it in the best form possible to anyone who will listen and read.

~ Lyda G. Garcia - Dublin, Ohio ~

PROLOGUE

My writing began while growing up in Bruni, TX, as I was a freshman in high school. I was in Home Economics class and so looked forward to it daily.
Although, I had knowledge of cooking and baking at home, I loved this class. Not only did I learn extra hacks, shortcuts and ideas for cooking but also for sewing.
Growing up in an exceedingly small community, (it had only a few streets,) really held not much to do. Every day or so I was either cooking or baking something. Grandma was always there to help me. I would bake cakes, cookies, pies, and cooked all sorts of breakfast, lunch, and dinner meals. Not to mention the traditional tortillas, both corn and flour.
Grandma once suggested that I should write a cookbook with all the delicious goodies we would whip up just about every other day. Lost count of how many times I did jot down recipes in notebooks. This was one thing she always brought up for me to do.
My grandmother Consuelo lost her cancer battle 5 years ago on November 11th, 2015. And her words were music to my ears.
One day, as I sat just reminiscing on life and other stuff, I decided to write recipes again. This time to fulfill my grandmother's request. So, in September 2019, this journey began, and I feel that Grandma has been guiding me from Heaven through this.

El Sabor De Mi Cocina

I love to cook and bake. I am always looking for new ideas to make for friends and family. My television is usually on the cooking channels observing all the chefs who are displaying their favorites.

I chose a few of the many recipes I have for this – my first cookbook, of several to follow.

I hope this book brings joy, pleasure, and FLAVOR to your kitchens, as it has to mine!!
~~ Connie

In Loving Memory of My Grandparents
Carlos & Consuelo Perez
(Mache & Chelo)

Gracias por la crianza que me dieron!

Thank you for bringing me up to be
who I am today!

El Sabor De Mi Cocina

Main Dishes

El Sabor De Mi Cocina

Fidello Con Chile

When I was growing up in Bruni, TX., my grandmother Consuelo would make this for us kids. We absolutely loved it. And we still crave it today. This, to me, could be an all-time meal. We already knew what she was going to make for dinner when she would send one of us outdoors with a little bowl to pick Pequin from the wild bush she had out back. She would then serve it with a side of her delicious, refried beans and homemade tortillas. Her tortillas were always on the gordita (chunky) side. Yes, it is deliciously delicious.   Recipe by ~Grandma Consuelo D. Perez+

Ingredients:

1 Box Q & Q Vermicelli (fidello de la cajita amarilla)

1 Tsp Chile Pequin (molido en molcajete)

1 Tsp Cominos (cumin)

1 to 2 Garlic cloves (powdered is good too)

1 Pinch of ground black pepper

1 Can of tomato sauce

Cooking oil for browning

All spices including Pequin should be grounded in molcajete

El Sabor De Mi Cocina

In a cooking pan on medium heat, add some cooking oil and bring it to a sizzling stage. Next, add box of fidello, stirring it consistently until it is lightly to golden brown. Add cumin, garlic, pepper and chile Pequin; stir quickly. Add enough HOT water to cover fidello. Bring to a slight boil and add whole can of tomato sauce. Add a little table salt to taste. Continue cooking on medium heat about 10-15 minutes, adding more water as needed to keep in soup consistency by ¼ cupsful at a time.

Note: Before starting the cooking, process make sure (if you want) to use a molcajete to crush and grind all your spices mentioned above. This way, it is already – ready for you to add to the browned fidello.

COMO DICE EL DICHO:

"CUANDO NO LLUEVE – TRUENA"

El Sabor De Mi Cocina

Carne Picada Con Papas

Grandma Consuelo D. Perez+

Traditionally, this dish is an all-time favorite in every Mexican residence. I have not yet met a family that does not know what this is. It is the normal, an average meal that will satisfy everyone's taste buds. Of course, the outcome of this is based on each individual cook. As the ingredients vary on other people's tastes. Meanwhile, this is the way my grandmother taught me. Simple y sencillo – simple and easy.

Ingredients:

1 Lb. Hamburger Meat

1 Can Whole Kernel Corn (water included)

1 Whole Tomato (diced)

½ Small Onion (diced)

2 Medium Potatoes (Peeled)

1 Tsp Cumin

½ Tsp Ground Peppercorns

2-3 Garlic Cloves (or 2 tsp ground)

1 Tsp Table Salt

1 Can Tomato Sauce

El Sabor De Mi Cocina

¼ Cup Chopped Fresh Cilantro

Cooking Oil

Procedure:

Brown potatoes and set aside. Brown the hamburger meat, drain the excess fat. Add onions, tomatoes, and sauté for about 10 minutes. Add all spices, cumin, peppercorn, salt and garlic. Stir occasionally for 5 minutes. Add can of diced tomatoes, juice and all. Stir slightly. Add can of whole kernel corn including its juice. Stir slightly. Add can of tomato sauce and cook down for 15-20 minutes. (if it starts to get too dry you can add another cup of water to keep it from absorbing dry) Next, add the fresh cilantro and let simmer another 10-15 minutes, since the potatoes have already been precooked.

COMO DICE EL DICHO:

"NO PUEDES VOLVER ATRAS Y CAMBIAR EL PRINCIPIO, PERO PUEDES COMENZAR DONDE ESTAS Y CAMBIAR EL FINAL"

El Sabor De Mi Cocina

Chicken Flautas

Ingredients:

4 Chicken Breasts (skinned, boiled & Shredded)

12 White Corn Tortillas

Cooking Oil

Cumin

Garlic

Salt & Pepper

(all spices are added to taste)

Sour Cream

Avocado Slices

Procedure:

Set shredded chicken aside. On medium-high heat sauté each of the 12 tortillas to a semi soft texture; set aside. Next, fill and roll tortilla with 2-3 tsp of shredded chicken mixture. Lay seam flat down on plate to avoid unrolling. Next bring frying pan back to medium-high heat and place 4 rolled & filled tortillas at a time, flat down in the hot oil to seal crisp. Turn gently to avoid oil splatter and burns. Cook until crispy golden brown all the way around. Serve with a dollop of sour cream on top and a side of lettuce, tomato, and avocado slices. Perhaps a side of Mexican rice to make it more delicious.

Enjoy!!

COMO DICE EL DICHO:

"LA VIDA ES MUY SIMPLE, PERO NOS EMPENAMOS EN HACERLA DIFICIL"

Fried Bacon - Sausage Kielbasa & Cabbage

This recipe here comes as a specialty from the state of Michigan. I worked at an adult foster care home for about 5 years. I took care of 11 mentally challenged ladies there. My boss was always cooking on the weekends and sending over to us during the cold winter afternoons. This was something I had never tasted. I had each of the 3, bacon, sausage and cabbage before but never in this concoction. But, once I tasted it, I kept making it for my home.

Ingredients:

1 Green Cabbage Head

2 Packages of Bacon (your choice)

1 Package Kielbasa (Sliced)

1 (8) oz Sour Cream

2 Tbsp Butter

Salt & Pepper (to taste)

Garlic (to taste)

Lemon Pepper (to taste)

Chili Powder (to taste & enough to redden)

Procedure:

Before Hand: shred cabbage, rinse/pat dry and dice bacon

El Sabor De Mi Cocina

In a large frying skillet add the diced-up bacon after allowing skillet to heat up on medium heat. Fry up to be crispy enough. Once done, scoop out of skillet and set aside in a dish. Toss in the same fat to cook, the kielbasa and cook down enough to be browned. Repeat scoop out and place in that same dish with the fried bacon to mix. Fold in the shredded cabbage and cook down until tender enough. Next add the cooked down bacon and kielbasa; stir. Add the spices; salt, garlic, ground cumin, lemon pepper and chili powder, stir. Continue cooking until cabbage is colored some in the chili powder.

*Note: Add a tablespoon or 2 of butter, just to upgrade the taste. Once done and removed from the skillet to the serving dish, add a dollop of sour cream if desired.

COMO DICE EL DICHO:

"NO MALGASTES TU TIEMPO, PUES DE ESA MATERIA ESTA FORMADA LA VIDA"

Taco Casserole

Ingredients:

2 Lb. Ground Beef (cooked & crumbled)

2 Packets Taco Seasoning

½ Bag Crushed Doritos (big bag)

8 Oz Cream Cheese (room temperature)

½ Cup Salsa

2 Cups Cheddar Cheese (shredded & divided)

2 Cups Shredded Lettuce

2 Cups Diced Tomato (diced canned is good too)

Taco Sauce

Sour Cream

Procedure:

Grease a 9x13" baking dish, add crushed Doritos to the bottom of the pan. Cook ground beef, add taco seasoning; cook as directed on the packet.

Spoon ground beef onto the crushed Doritos, spreading evenly. In a medium sized mixing bowl, beat cream cheese, slowly; add in salsa. Once thoroughly mixed, top ground beef with cream cheese mixture.

Top with ½ cup shredded cheese. Bake at 350 degrees for 25-30 minutes, or until hot and bubbly. When done and out of the oven, top with cheese and shredded lettuce, diced tomatoes and remaining 1/2 cup cheese.

Top with sour cream and add (drizzle) taco sauce.

COMO DICE EL DICHO:

"LA VIDA NO SIEMPRE SON TRENES A LOS QUE HAY QUE SUBIR, A VECES SON ESTACIONES EN LAS QUE HAY QUE BAJAR"

El Sabor De Mi Cocina

Italy Meatloaf

Traditionally, MEATLOAF is basically MEATLOAF...right? Well, this is a little different in ingredients. This recipe was shared by one of my strongest supporters for this cookbook. Since I mentioned it to her, she started gathering some of her favorite recipes so that I can add them here. She is my cousin, Carolina Y. Rocha – Parkman, Friendswood, TX. (Our Mothers are sisters)

Ingredients:

1 Yellow Onion, diced

1 Red pepper, diced & fire roasted

Olive oil for sauteing

5 Cloves of garlic

1 Vine ripened tomato, diced

1 Tbsp dried Italian seasoning

1 Egg

¾ Cup tomato sauce

1 Tsp. Worcestershire sauce

1 ¼ Lb. ground beef or turkey

½ Cup Italian seasoned breadcrumbs

¼ Tsp black pepper

2 Tbsp parmesan cheese, shredded

Procedure:

Heat a skillet with enough oil to cover the bottom of the pan over medium to low heat, add onion and pepper, sauté until tender. Add garlic, sauté until fragrant; add tomato and Italian seasoning, sauté another 3-4 minutes. Set aside to cool. Preheat oven to 400 degrees F. In a large bowl whisk together egg, 1/3 cup tomato sauce, and Worcestershire. Add ground meat, breadcrumbs, black pepper, parmesan & sautéed veggies. Combine with fork; mix in 1 cup of mozzarella cheese. In a large greased roasting pan, form the meat into a loaf. Spread the remaining ½ cup sauce over top and sprinkle with remaining ½ cup mozzarella. Bake about 45 minutes or until no longer pink in the middle Let sit 5 minutes before serving. Delicious…do not forget to share your leftovers!

COMO DICE EL DICHO:

"EL TIEMPO QUE SE DISFRUTA ES EL VERDADERO TIEMPO VIVIDO"

Tia Ana's Enchilada Casserole

Everyone is used to Enchiladas...whether they are the original enchilada sauced, rojas, callejeras, enmoladas, suizas. Tia (aunt) Ana made this dish on weekends. I remember spending the weekend at her and my Tio's home as she would announce that she was going to be making this. It is prepared different but vastly has just about the same ingredients. – Ana M. Perez, Hebbronville/Orange Grove, TX.

Ingredients:

2 Lbs. Hamburger Meat

2 Cans Cream of Chicken

2 Cans Enchilada Sauce (preferably Old El Paso Medium)

1 -2 tbsp chili powder

30 Count Corn Tortillas

Cheese (mild cheddar)

Procedure:

Brown meat, when done, add chili powder and cook 5 minutes, then add cans of cream of chicken & cans of enchilada sauce. Mix and heat until warm enough to wet the tortillas in that same sauce. Layer them in a 9x13" pan alternating the cheese & meat, in layers to start the casserole layout. Once you run out of tortillas pour the remaining sauce mixture over the top. Next, top with the remaining shredded cheddar cheese. Bake in oven at 350 degrees F for 20-30 minutes or until cheese is completely melted.

COMO DICE EL DICHO:

"QUIEN NO SE A CAIDO NUNCA, NO TIENE IDEA JUSTA DEL ESFUERZO QUE HAY QUE HACER PARA MANTENERSE DE PIE"

Creamy Garlic Mushroom & Bacon

Carolina Y. Rocha - Parkman

Ingredients:
8 Oz. bacon, cut into strips
2 Tbsp butter
26 Oz. brown mushrooms, washed and dried (pat dry with a paper towel)
1 Tbsp Olive oil
¼ Cup dry white wine or chicken broth stock
6 Cloves garlic, finely chopped
1½ Cups heavy cream or evaporated milk
1 Tbsp fresh chopped parsley
1 Tsp fresh chopped thyme
Salt & pepper to season
½ Cup fresh shredded or grated mozzarella cheese
¼ Cup fresh shredded or grated parmesan cheese

Procedure:

Fry the bacon in a large oven safe skillet over medium heat until crispy. Use a slotted spoon to transfer to a paper towel lined plate so it can soak up some of the oil. Set it aside.

In the same pan, melt the butter. Add the mushrooms, drizzle with oil and mix through, scraping up any browned bits from the bottom of the pan. Fry for 2-3 minutes to lightly brown mushrooms and release their juices if any.

Pour in the wine or broth and let reduce for 2 minutes, while occasionally stirring.

Preheat your broiler or oven grill

Add in the garlic and stir it through for a minute, until fragrant. Pour in the cream and herbs. Reduce the heat to low. Gently simmer until tender for about 4-5 minutes, and sauce is slightly thickened. Season with salt and pepper. Add the bacon back in and give everything a good mix to combine all the flavors together. Top the mushrooms with the mozzarella and parmesan cheese. Broil until cheese is melted and bubbly and mushrooms are done to your liking. Just about 3-5 minutes – serve warm.

COMO DICE EL DICHO:

"NO PROMETAS CUANDO ESTES FELIZ, NO RESPONDAS CUANDO ESTES ENOJADO Y NO DECIDAS CUANDO ESTES TRISTE"

Mini Meat Loaves

Connie Guerrero Palacios

Ingredients:

1 Egg

¾ Cup Milk

1 Cup Chopped Onion

½ Cup Dry oatmeal

1 Tsp salt

1 Lb. ground beef

½ Cup ketchup

¼ cup brown sugar

1 Tsp mustard

Procedure:

Mix all ingredients together in order given. Shape into 4 equal loaves. Or use 1 whole loaf, however you feel would benefit your serving needs.

Topping:

Combine ½ cup ketchup with ¼ cup brown sugar and 1 tsp mustard, mix well. Top each loaf completely and bake in oven at 350 degrees F, for 45 minutes.

Note: You can use ground turkey but omit or reduce the milk.

COMO DICE EL DICHO:

"SI NO TE GUSTA ALGO, CAMBIALO. SI NO LO PUEDES CAMBIAR, CAMBIA TU ACTITUD"

Wella's Enchiladas

Grandma Consuelo D. Perez+

To this day, I am very picky on enchiladas. This is the way I grew up eating them. So, this is the way, I prefer them now. Sometimes I will make them an easier way, but to have them like this is like going back to my childhood growing up in Bruni, TX.

Ingredients:

1 Package 30 count white corn tortillas
2 Cans Wolf Chili with beans, mild or hot
1 Block or package (x2) shredded cheese
1 Medium onion, diced
1 Cup vegetable or corn oil for frying the tortillas
2 to 3 Tsp Chili powder, Gebhart (preferably)

El Sabor De Mi Cocina

Procedure:

Heat skillet on medium heat. Add oil and bring to a hot sizzle. Add chili powder stirring enough with a whisk so that clumping is prevented. Sauté corn tortillas; one at a time; semi crunchy. Not too soft either, just enough to roll later without them tearing apart. Once they are all done, set aside. Now, roll them with cheese and onions (if desired).

Next, start laying them all in a pan and top with remaining cheese and onions. Pour over them, the chili with beans. Make sure all the rolled enchiladas are covered with the chili. Top with remaining cheese and onions, there is any left.

Bake in preheated oven at 350 degrees F for 30-45 minutes or until bubbly melted cheese is visible.

Note: You do not have to use the onions. I do because this just the way my Grandma would make this dish for us.

COMO DICE EL DICHO:

"A LO MEJOR NO TIENES LA VIDA QUE SONASTE, PERO POSIBLEMENTE TIENES LA VIDA QUE MUCHOS SUENAN"

Vaquero Burger

Veronica "Ronnie" Guerrero - Gonzales, Falfurrias, TX.

My cousin Ronnie is a very challenge taking lady. She is always finding the way to progress in life and make a living like all of us in some sort of way. Well, she owned a little lunch stand in Falfurrias, TX where this burger was one of her menu's top sellers. It is one heck of a burger if you ask around. Delicious by far. This recipe makes 4 burgers.

Ingredients:

1 1/2 Lbs. 80% lean 20% fat ground beef or ground chuck
4 eggs
1 Tbsp. Worcestershire sauce
1½ Tsp seasoning salt
1 Tsp garlic powder
½ Tsp ground black pepper

*Optional: 4 slices of pepper jack cheese
4 Hamburger buns
4 Jalapenos, sliced
Bacon
Mushrooms

Procedure:

Preheat grill to 375-degree F (medium/high). In a large bowl, add beef, Worcestershire sauce, seasoning salt, garlic powder, pepper and use your hands to mix all the ingredients together until they are all combined.

Divide the meat mixture into 4th's; taking ¼ of the meat mixture & using your hands to press it in the shape of a hamburger patty. That is about ¾ inch thick. Make an indentation in the middle of the patty to prevent it from bulging in the center, as it is cooking. Repeat process with remaining 3 parts of meat. Place patties to cook on the preheated grill cooking about 5 minutes on each side. Cook bacon on grill with the fat left over and mushrooms from patties. Once done, place bacon (3-4 strips) and mushrooms over patty. Cook an egg to your liking; fried, over easy, sunny side up, or scrambled and place on top of bacon/mushroom. Then top burger with bun, add mustard or mayo if desired.

Note: Jalapenos can be served on the side or sliced with mushrooms and bacon.

COMO DICE EL DICHO:

"LA VIDA ES MUY SIMPLE, PERO NOS EMPENAMOS EN HACERLA DIFICIL"

Menudo

Ingredients:

8 Lbs. Regular tribe (pansa) precut to bite size pieces
7 Lbs. Honeycomb tribe, also precut to bite size pieces

1 Big can white hominy

1 bottle Gebhart chili powder (use your judgement to desired red consistency)

3 Tbsp whole oregano/menudo spice
8 garlic cloves
3 Tbsp peppercorns
6 Tsp whole cumin
1 cup white vinegar

Salt to taste

Note: grind all the spices except for the oregano/menudo spice in the molcajete or food processor

Procedure:
Fill sink with water ¾ full and put in both tribes. Add about 1 cup of white vinegar, mix well, let soak about 30 minutes toss turning a few times. This is to help clean the tribe before cooking. Release the soaking water and with faucet running give it a good rinse about another 10 minutes to make sure the tribe is clean.

While this is going on, prepare your roaster with water for cooking on high to get water boiling quicker. Next strain tribe pour into roaster letting cook about 1 hour before adding the spices previously ground in the molcajete. Add water to molcajete or food processor to get the excess spices out. Let cook on 300 (roaster setting) 4 to 5 hours checking up on it. Making sure the tribe is getting tender (using your judgement) and always has enough water. To prevent it from evaporating too much.

At this point, add oregano/menudo spice, let cook another 1 to 2 hours. Once tender enough add your hominy juices and all. This will help your menudo to thicken some.

El Sabor De Mi Cocina

Whisk in the chili powder making sure there isn't any clumping as you are pouring it into the kettle slowly. Add salt to taste. Let cook another 45 minutes just to make sure the chili powder color has saturated into the meat and hominy.

Note: If you plan to add beef or pork feet, rinse well and add them to the roaster before you add the tribes. They take longer to cook. Or you can also cook them separately and when the menudo is ½ way done, you can add them to the roaster then. This way they will not fall apart.

COMO DICE EL DICHO:

"POR MUY LARGA QUE SEA LA TORMENTA, EL SOL SIEMPRE VUELVE A BRILLAR ENTRE LAS NUBES"

El Sabor De Mi Cocina

Cheesy Hash Browns

Ingredients:

1 Package shredded hash browns
1 can (10 3/4 oz) cream of chicken soup
¾ Cup sour cream
¼ Cup chopped onion
¼ Cup butter or margarine, melted
Topping:
1½ Cup cornflakes, coarsely crushed
2 Tbsp butter or margarine, melted

Procedure:

(9x13 inch or 8x8 inch baking dish can be used)

Heat oven to 350-degree F, spray bottom of baking dish with nonstick cooking spray. In a large bowl combine all hash brown ingredients; mix well. Spread into prepared baking dish. In small bowl stir together topping ingredients. Spread topping evenly over hash browns. Bake 45 minutes or until hash browns are tender.

COMO DICE EL DICHO:

"SOMOS EL FRUTO DE NUESTRAS PALABRAS, LA CONSECUENCIA DE NUESTROS ACTOS"

Fluffy White Rice

This is my traditional white rice that I use especially when I make my egg rolls.

Ingredients:

1½ Cups raw white rice (Riceland)

1½ Tsp salt

1½ Tbsp butter

3 to 4 Cups water

Procedure:

In a medium saucepan, combine 3 cups cold water with rice, salt and butter. Bring to a rolling boil, uncovered.

Reduce heat; simmer, covered for about 10 to 15 minutes. Or until the rice is tender, and all the water is absorbed.

Fluff up with a fork.

COMO DICE EL DICHO:

"CAERSE MIL VECES Y LEVANTARSE DE NUEVO - EN ESO CONSISTE LA VIDA"

Jean Ann's Quick Chili

Ingredients:

1 pound of hamburger meat

1 package chili seasoning

1 can of chili beans

Procedure:

Fry up the hamburger meat, drain off the extra fat. Add the chili seasoning, and the can of chili beans. Juice and all. Let cook down on low heat for about 30 minutes. Enjoy with a fresh batch of corn bread.

COMO DICE EL DICHO:

"NUNCA DIGAS – NUNCA"

Connie's Egg Rolls

Ingredients:

Oil (for deep frying)
1 Package egg roll wraps
1 Lb. Hamburger meat
2 Cups shredded cabbage
2 Cups bean sprouts (fresh if possible)
   Or canned, well drained and rinsed
2 scrambled eggs
2 Tbsp soy sauce
1 Cup small egg noodles (optional) cooked
Sweet & Sour sauce for dipping (your choice)

Procedure:

In a large pan, cook to brown the hamburger meat. Drain the fat, add the shredded cabbage and cook a bit for 10 minutes on medium heat. Enough to sauté. Add bean sprouts, cook about 5 minutes. Add 2 tbsp soy sauce to the entire mixture. Add the scrambled eggs and mix well. Cook another 5 minutes. Remove from heat and set aside.

Egg rolls:

Place eggroll wrap with a corner facing you (diamond style). Place 3-4 tbsp more or less of mixture in center; avoiding overflow. This may rip and spill while frying. Moisten a dab just enough to seal edges. If you are not certain on how to wrap this, you can always check it out on YouTube or ask Google. Basically, all you are going to do is fold over the mixture that corner flap, then fold over the right and fold over the left and roll to finish the seal. Next deep fry 2 minutes on each side until golden brown. Set on paper towel to absorb excess oil.

*Serve with a side of White or Fried Rice and sweet & Sour Sauce for dipping of eggroll.

COMO DICE EL DICHO:

"NADIE EN ESTA VIDA ES PERFECTO, ASI QUE ACEPTATE TAL Y COMO ERES"

Southern Fried Salmon Patties

Ingredients:

1 (14) oz can salmon

¼ Cup onion, finely chopped

¼ Cup Cornmeal

¼ Cup flour

1 Egg

3 Tbsp mayonnaise

Procedure:

Open salmon and drain thoroughly. Place drained salmon in mixing bowl and flake evenly with a fork. Add onion, cornmeal, flour, mayonnaise & egg. Stir until well blended. Slightly, trying to avoid it smashing too much. You do not want it to look like a mush. You want for your mixture to have some chunky texture.

Shape the mixture into patties. The size of an average burger or less will be perfect. Cook in oil on skillet over medium heat until browned on each side. Turn once while frying.

Note: The mayonnaise helps the patties hold their shape & keeps them from being too dry.

COMO DICE EL DICHO:

"HOY SON ERRORS, MANANA SON EXPERIENCIAS"

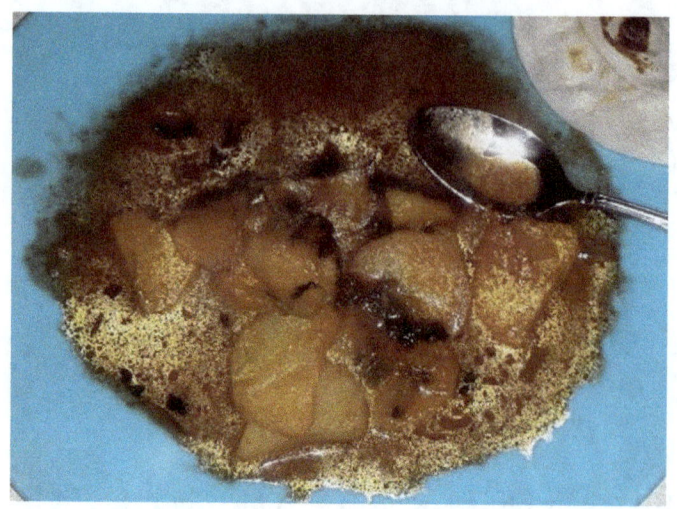

Papas Caldudas

This is also a dish we ate often as kids. Grandma would whip up a stack of homemade flour tortillas and these papitas. We would have it with refried beans and sun brewed tea. We had simple meals that filled our tummies to a complete satisfaction.

Ingredients:

5 Medium potatoes, cleaned and peeled

1 Small onion, diced

1 Large tomato, diced

1 Serrano pepper, sliced/diced

1 (8) oz can tomato sauce

El Sabor De Mi Cocina

¼ Cup chopped cilantro

8 to 16 oz water for cook down

Salt & pepper to taste

Cumin, to taste

Garlic, to taste

Procedure:

Cut cleaned potatoes to your desired choice, diced or rounded slices. Fry as if frying for French fries, not completely done though. Remove most of the cooking oil, leaving about 1 to 2 tsp for the cooking of the remaining ingredients. Add the diced onions, tomatoes, serrano; quickly stir. Cook down about 5 minutes. Add spices and salt/pepper to taste; stir. Add 8 oz water, you will hear sizzling, stir lightly. Add can of tomato sauce, let cook down 10 minutes. Add more water if you feel you want it soupier. At this point, add the ¼ cup of cilantro; finish cooking another 15 minutes. Serve with corn or homemade flour tortillas.

COMO DICE EL DICHO:

"SONRIE A LA VIDA, NO DEJES QUE LA VIDA SE RIA DE TI"

Conejito Frito
(Fried Rabbit)

To many it is like, yuck, but to many people, this is a delicacy. Fried rabbit is so delicious. It tastes just like chicken, white meat. I loved to go to the ranch with my grandpa to hunt rabbit. Back in like the late 80-90's, to be more precise. I remember we would get home with a sacksful of rabbit. Sometimes, I would count to 30 to 40 rabbits. Grandma would help Grandpa skin and cut the rabbit, then to the freezer they would go. On a hot Sunday afternoon, Grandma would cook up the Fried Rabbit feast for us all. And we would stay hungry for more.

This recipe here will be the equivalency of 1 rabbbit...you can double or triple the rabbits to make more. At our home, 1 rabbit was not enough. Grandma would have up to 4 plates piled up with the fried rabbit at our dinner table.

Ingredients:

1 Young rabbit, cut into pieces
2 Cups buttermilk
1 Medium size onion, finely sliced
3 Garlic cloves, diced or on the molcajete
1 Tsp paprika
2 Cups all-purpose flour
1 Tsp onion powder
1 Tsp garlic powder
Salt and pepper to taste
2 - 3 Cups vegetable oil for the frying

El Sabor De Mi Cocina

Procedure:

Soak the rabbit overnight in the buttermilk, along the onion, garlic, herbs, and paprika.

When ready to start your cooking the next day, drain in a colander, leaving some herbs on the rabbit. In a large plastic or zip lock bag or bowl, mix the flour with the powders, onion, cayenne and the salt and pepper. Set aside

Next, heat the oil in a large, skillet over medium high heat or until a pinch of flour starts to sizzle when dropped in the hot oil. But make sure it is not so hot as to the oil to be smoking.

Place the rabbit pieces in the bag with the flour mixture and shake to coat all the pieces. Do this with a few pieces at a time. You do not want to overload the pan. Start dropping them into the pan to cook. Fry on each side at least 10 minutes. Making sure they are not burning the flour coating. If this starts to happen, simply lower the heat setting. Make sure there is always enough oil to keep the rabbit cooking at a floating consistency.

El Sabor De Mi Cocina

When the 10 minutes are up at each side, remove the rabbit from the skillet and place it on a wire rack or over paper towels. Season it immediately with salt and pepper to taste, to help keep the crispiness. This was always served with a side of Mexican rice and simple side salad of lettuce, tomato, cucumbers and diced onions. The topping for the salad was always freshly squeezed lemon juice. And of course, the homemade tortillas.

COMO DICE EL DICHO:

"AFORTUNADO EN EL JUEGO – DESAFORTUNADO EN EL AMOR"

El Sabor De Mi Cocina

Pollo En Mole

Ingredients:

1 chicken cut up in 8 pieces
8 oz Jar Dona Maria mole mix (trust me this is a much faster way)
½ cup peanut butter smooth
1 teas garlic powder
half of liquid broth from boiling the chicken

Procedure:

Boil chicken (enough water to cover about 3 inches over chicken)

once chicken is cooked add 2 cups chicken broth to blender set aside

to remaining broth with chicken add jar of mole mix stir

in blender you've set aside with broth add peanut butter and garlic powder blend to liquify then add blender mixture to chicken in pot and mix to combine simmer till all is hot you want a gravy consistency and serve with Mexican rice.

COMO DICE EL DICHO:

"QUIEN ME CERRO LAS PUERTAS, ME DIO LAS LLAVES DE MI TALENTO"

Carne Guisada

An all-time favorite dish of one of my brothers. My brother Rene, he just loves this. He and my other 2 brothers are over the road truck drivers and when they come home from being out for several weeks at a time, they request of certain foods to eat. Well, Rene's favorite is carne Guisada. He really does not mind who makes it. As long as its carne Guisada. Ahh, y que no falten las tortillas de harina!!

Ingredients:

2 large garlic cloves, peeled and minced
1 Serrano Chile, minced, plus additional sliced Serrano for garnish (optional)
15 whole black peppercorns
¼ teaspoon cumin seeds
2 tablespoons canola oil
1½ pounds bottom round steak or beef chuck, meat cut into ½-inch cubes
1 large white onion, diced

El Sabor De Mi Cocina

1½ teaspoons all-purpose flour
1 teaspoon salt
2 medium potatoes, diced
Fresh cilantro leaves (optional)

Procedure:

Use a molcajete or food processor to mash the garlic, mince the chile, peppercorns and cumin seeds into a smooth paste. Add ¼ cup water and mash until the paste is mixed into the water. Transfer the mixture to a measuring cup. Heat 1 tablespoon oil in a large pot over medium heat. Add half the steak and cook, stirring occasionally, until browned on all sides, about 8 minutes. Transfer the browned meat to a plate and repeat with the remaining oil and meat. Bring back the browned meat to the large pot, then add the onion and cook, stirring occasionally, until soft and tender, usually about 3 minutes. (The trick to the gravy here is the onion itself will produce a thickening to the broth and help make it into the gravy) Sprinkle the flour and 1 teaspoon salt over the beef and stir to incorporate, then add the blended garlicky liquid and just enough water to barely cover the meat (about 2 cups). Bring up the heat to medium-high and use a spoon to scrape the bottom of the large pot, releasing any browned bits. Bring the liquid to a boil, then immediately lower the heat so that it cooks at a low simmer. Cover the pot and cook until the meat is tender, 1 ½ to 2 hours. Remove the lid and stir in the diced potatoes & cilantro if using for the added flavor. Let it cook, stirring occasionally, until the potatoes are tender, and the sauce has thickened slightly, about 15 minutes. Season to taste with salt. Serve with hot tortillas.

COMO DICE EL DICHO:

El Sabor De Mi Cocina

"LO QUE MORTIFICA – NI SE RECUERDA NI SE PLATICA"
<u>Carne Guisada en Salsa Verde</u>

This recipe has been added at the very last minute, right about submitting to publisher. This was a request from one of my customers at my place of work. I shared with him my news on the publicity of my book and he asked if I had a version for this. Well, yes, indeed. So here you go!

Ingredients:
2 pounds beef (your choice of cut, I like to use roast plank) cut into small chunks
1-pound tomatillo or green tomato
1 whole stalk of fresh cilantro
½ onion
2 garlic cloves, peeled, diced and pureed in the molcajete or food processor
Cooking oil about 3 tbsp
Salt to taste
1 tsp Comino (cumin)
¼ tsp ground black pepper
Chile Serrano to taste if you want a spicy sauce. If not do not use any.

Procedure:
In a big enough kettle, to fit all the tomatillos or tomatoes, bring them to boil along the serrano if you will be using it.

El Sabor De Mi Cocina

Once boiled set aside to cool some. Now that it is cooled enough, bring it to a blender to blend slightly enough to get a puree. Set aside until ready to add to the meat mixture.

Bring onto a large skillet about 3 tbsp of cooking oil and let it get hot.
Add in the cut up small chunks of meat and cook all the way through. Stirring enough to prevent the meat from sticking to the pan. When the meat is halfway cooked, add in the onion, chopped and tossed in with the meat to cook and help it thicken the tomatillo sauce to cook for 5 minutes.
Now, you can add the tomatillo sauce, spices – including garlic, Comino (cumin), pepper and salt to taste. Let that simmer on low heat for 20 minutes. Stirring it to prevent sticking. Serve with a side of Mexican or white rice and frijoles (beans).

COMO DICE EL DICHO:
"DE GRANO EN GRANO - LLENA LA GAILLINA EL BUCHE"

Enfrijoladas

Ingredients:
2 (15) ounce cans of black beans
Chipotle pepper in adobo sauce (add depending on how spicy you like it - recommended to use is 3 peppers with the sauce)

½ Cup chopped onions
1½ Tsp minced garlic
¼ Tsp oregano
1 Tbsp olive oil
12 White corn tortillas
8 ounces queso fresco (cotija works best)
For Topping:
Chopped cilantro, sour cream, red salsa

Procedure:
In a large blender, I add the black beans, undrained, chipotle peppers, onions, garlic and the oregano. I blend it until the black bean sauce is silky smooth.
Next, heat a medium pot or skillet over medium high heat. Add the olive oil and pour in the black bean sauce. Cook it and stirring it frequently, until the mixture is hot and bubbly.

If the sauce gets too thick, just add a little water or broth, and mix it in. just be careful and do not add too much water or it will be too watery.

Heat up the corn tortillas on the skillet or in the microwave for about 1 minute, until warm and pliable.

To assemble the enfrijoladas, dip each tortilla into the black bean sauce. Transfer it to a plate and fill with cheese. Roll it up like an enchilada or fold it over like a taco.

Serve immediately with fresh cilantro, sour cream and the red salsa.

COMO DICE EL DICHO:

"RENGO RENGO, PERO VENGO"

Liebre Guisada
(Jack Rabbit Stew)

You must prepare this a day before so that all the spices are soaked up and the taste of the wild will not be so harsh. At the end, this is a delicious delicacy.

Ingredients:

¼ Cup vegetable oil

3 Garlic cloves

1 Medium onion

2 Bay leaves (Oja de Laurel)

1 Jack Rabbit (of course skinned and cleaned)

Pinch of salt and pepper

½ of ¼ Cup Vinegar

2 Medium tomatoes

3 Carrots, sliced

½ Cup all-purpose flour

Procedure:

In a large pan, add the cut-up Jack Rabbit, carrots, onion the spices including the bay leaf. Also add the salt and pepper and the vinegar. Let it soak up in the fridge for at least 12 hours.

Next day when you are ready to cook your stew, take the pieces of meat out and separate the vegetables. Reserve the broth the raw meat was soaking in. Add this broth to a saucepan and let it come to a boil. Once it is boiled, bring it to a colander and strain it. You just want the plain broth.

Add this broth and the meat to a pan where you will begin to cook your stew. Cook it down for about 1 hour and 20 minutes. Keep the lid on making sure it does not empty out of the broth. Keep it at a low to medium heat setting. Once the meat is soft and tender, add about 2 tablespoons of red chili powder and cook another 5 minutes.

Brown in the vegetable oil a ½ cup of all-purpose flour then add it slowly as you are stirring to prevent clumping in the stew. It may require some water to thin it out some. It is a gravy form. Continue to cook on low heat for another 15 minutes, just enough to cook the flour you just added for the gravy.

COMO DICE EL DICHO:

"BARBA DE TRES COLORES, NO LA TRAEN SINO LOS TRAIDORES"

Pozole de Puerco
(Pork Pozole)

This process is the same for Pozole de Pollo - Chicken Pozole. Of course, all you do is substitute the pork for chicken breast pieces.

2 pounds of pork cut into medium sized cubes
¼ Cup of Gebhart Chili Powder
1 or 2 Cans of hominy
6 cloves of garlic
Salt and Pepper to taste
½ onion
1 teaspoon of oregano
1 teaspoon of cumin
2 bay leaves (Oja de Laurel)
2 Cups Chopped radish, thinly sliced
Lime to taste
1 Cup chopped cabbage
   chopped cilantro
1 chopped onion

Procedure:

Cook the pork meat in sufficient water, making sure that the pork is completely covered with water. Add 1 clove of garlic, 1/4 piece of an onion (not diced), the bay leaves, salt and pepper. After it has cooked down, set aside 1/2 cup of the broth from cooking the pork.

Once the meat is cooked, remove the bay leaf, onion, and garlic clove, and add the hominy and bring to a boil for 15 minutes. Once the hominy is cooking, add the chili powder stirring it continuously. Avoiding it to clump. You may need or want to add a little more, I like to eat it very red. But it is up to your taste and like.

Blend the remaining 5 cloves of garlic, another 1/4 piece of the onion, the cumin, the salt, the pepper, the 1/2 cup of broth that was set aside in step 1 above, and 1/2 cup of hominy (to thicken the sauce) in a blender until completely blended.

Once the above mixture is blended, strain the mixture and add the strained liquid to the boiling pot with the pork and water. Season with oregano and add salt to taste. Let boil 15 minutes longer.

Serve hot, topped with chopped lettuce, onions, radishes, and a few drops of lime and finally the homemade tortillas.

COMO DICE EL DICHO:

"MAS HACE EL LOBO CALLANDO, QUE EL PERRO LADRANDO"

El Sabor De Mi Cocina

Cheesy Chicken Fritters

Ingredients:

1-1/2 lbs. Chicken breasts (about 3 large)
2 large eggs
1/3 cup mayonnaise
1/3 cup all-purpose flour or cornstarch for gluten free
4 oz mozzarella cheese (1 1/3 cups shredded)
1½ tbsp chopped fresh dill or dried if available
½ tsp salt to taste
1/8 tsp ground pepper to taste
2 tbsp extra light olive oil to sauté (or any high heat cooking oil)
Ingredients for Garlic Aioli Dip (optional)
1/3 cup mayonnaise
1 garlic clove pressed
½ tbsp lemon juice
¼ tsp salt
1/8 tsp black pepper

Procedure:

Using a sharp knife, dice chicken into cubed thick pieces and place them in a large mixing bowl. Trying chicken breasts partially frozen, it will be a little bit easier to slice.

Into the mixing bowl, add remaining batter, ingredients: 2 eggs, 1/3 cup mayonnaise, 1/3 cup flour, 1 1/3 cups shredded mozzarella, 1 ½ tbs dill, ½ tsp salt and 1/8 tsp black pepper, or season to taste.

Stir in the mixture until well combined, cover with plastic wrap and refrigerate 2 hours or overnight.

Heat a large nonstick pan over medium heat and add 2 tbsp oil. When oil is hot, add the chicken mixture a heaping tablespoon at a time. Slightly flatten out the tops with the back of your spoon and sauté uncovered 3-4 minutes on the first side or until outsides are golden brown and chicken is fully cooked through.

repeat with remaining fritters, adding more oil as needed

Dip:

To make Aioli (if using) combine all ingredients in a small bowl or measuring cup and stir.

Tip:

To test doneness, cut a fritter in half and the chicken should be completely white inside. If your chicken patty is browning too fast, adjust your heat down.

Tip 2:

Serve with a side of lettuce, tomatoes, lemon slices. Perhaps with some scallop potatoes as well.

COMO DICE EL DICHO:

"LA CLARIDAD CONSERVA LA AMISTAD"

El Sabor De Mi Cocina

King Ranch Beef Pasta

Ingredients:

1-pound pasta noodles of your choice

1-pound ground beef

2 cans rotel tomatoes

2 cans cheddar cheese soup

1 can cream of mushroom soup

1 can cream of chicken soup

1 tsp minced garlic

½ c diced onion

Chili powder, salt and pepper to taste.

Procedure:

Cook ground beef with onion, drain well, mix in remaining ingredients, heat and add to pasta. Top with grated cheddar cheese. Simple…pop in a preheated oven to 350 degrees for 30-45 minutes. Serve warm with a side of green beans and corn and some garlic bread.

COMO DICE EL DICHO:

"POR UN MAL VECINO - NO DESAGAS TU NIDO"

Garbage Soup

Ingredients:

1-pound ground beef
1 can hot rotel
1 can ranch style beans
1 can whole kernel corn
1 onion, diced
Salt & pepper to taste
Garlic powder & Cumin (1 tsp of each)
Water
1 can tomato sauce

Procedure:

In a medium deep-dish skillet, sauté the ground beef. Drain out all the fat, add garlic powder, cumin, diced onion and continue to sauté until the onion pieces are tender. Next, add can of hot rotel, stir. Let cook for about 2-3 minutes. Continue adding remaining ingredients; can of beans, can of corn (juice and all), and can of tomato sauce. Add 4 cups of water to make it soupy. Lastly, add salt and pepper to taste. I like to serve this dish with a side of fresh corn tortillas. To each their choice.

COMO DICE EL DICHO:

"EL CASADO DESCONTENTO – SIEMPRE VIVE CON TORMENTO"

Vaquero Stew

Ingredients:

1-pound tenderized skinless fajitas, cut into small pieces

1 can hot rotel

1 can ranch style beans

1 can whole kernel corn

1 onion, diced

Salt & pepper to taste

Garlic powder & Cumin (1 tsp of each)

Water

1 can tomato sauce

Procedure:

In a medium deep-dish skillet, sauté the beef fajitas. Drain out all the fat, add garlic powder, cumin, diced onion and continue to sauté until the onion pieces are tender. Next, add can of hot rotel, stir. Let cook for about 2-3 minutes. Continue adding remaining ingredients; can of beans, can of corn (juice and all), and can of tomato sauce. Add 4 cups of water to make it soupy.

Lastly, add salt and pepper to taste. I like to serve this dish with a side of fresh corn tortillas. To each their choice.

COMO DICE EL DICHO:

"MAS VALE UNA COLORADA - QUE CIEN DESCOLORIDAS"

Nopalitos en Salsa Con Chorizo

Ingredients:

8 ounces Mexican chorizo (I prefer to use the beef chorizo)

½ onion, diced

2 cups Nopalitos, previously cooked and thinly diced

1 medium russet potato peeled and sliced

Cilantro chopped, for garnish

3 roma tomatoes, diced

2 serrano peppers, diced

2 cloves garlic, sliced and diced

¼ cup cooking oil

1¾ cup chicken broth

1½ tsp Knorr chicken bouillon powder

1/3 tsp cumin

¼ tsp ground pepper

Salt to taste (if needed)

Procedure:

Heat a skillet to medium heat. Add ¼ cup of oil and let warm up for a few minutes. Add the onions, garlic, tomatoes, serrano peppers and let sauté for 5-6 minutes. Add the Nopalitos and sauté another 5 minutes, then add the chorizo (previously cooked) and stir about 3 minutes. Then add chicken broth into the skillet and bring to a boil about 6 minutes and reduce heat to simmer. While it is on simmer add the diced-up potatoes, Knorr bouillon and continue simmering until tendered. Garnish with cilantro and serve warm with a side of fresh homemade tortillas. (I prefer to add the cilantro while the Nopalitos are cooking down) Add a little water if needed to get a little sauce in it.

COMO DICE EL DICHO:

"SI TE DIGO QUE LA BURRA ES PINTA-ES QUE LOS PELOS LOS TRAIGO EN LA MANO"

Nopales a la Mexicana

Ingredients:

1 tbsp vegetable oil

2 cups Nopalitos diced and cooked

1/4 cup white onion diced

1 clove garlic chopped

2 serrano (or 1 jalapeno) peppers sliced and diced

1 cup tomato chopped

¼ cup cilantro

Salt and pepper to taste

Procedure:

Heat oil in a frying pan over a medium high heat. Once hot, add the onion and cook for a couple of minutes or until it starts to look transparent.

Stir in the serrano pepper and garlic clove and cook for about one minute.

Add the tomato and cook another 5 minutes; by this time, the tomatoes will start releasing their juices.

Finally, stir in the Nopalitos and the cilantro. Let it cook another 5 minutes to allow the flavors to blend in. If your sauce is too thick, add a little water to thin out some. Season with salt and pepper to taste. Serve warm with corn or flour tortillas.

COMO DICE EL DICHO:

"TANTO VA EL CANTARO AL AGUA –
HASTA QUE SE QUIEBRA"

Nopalitos con Huevo

2 Nopalito pads (makes about 1 cup)

2 cloves garlic, peeled, sliced and diced

Salt & pepper to taste

2 tbsp vegetable oil

½ small onion, peeled and diced

4 eggs, beaten (as per scrambled eggs)

1 tomato, diced

Corn/flour tortillas

Procedure:

Using a small sharp knife, clean the Nopalitos (cactus) by scraping off the thorns or spines from both sides if you chose to use the wild ones. Trim off the edges and any blemished areas. Wash well with cold water.

Next, slice and dice the paddle. Add to a medium saucepan and cook over medium heat keeping an eye on them so that they do not boil over. Add 1 tsp of salt and enough water to cover the Nopalitos. Bring to a rolling boil. Cook for about 20-25 minutes. You will notice they will turn palish in color when done.

Drain the Nopalitos and rinse well under very cold water. Rinse again as needed to rid the foam they create as they are being boiled.

In a skillet over medium heat, heat the oil and add the diced onions and cook until softened. Add the drained Nopalitos and cook for about 3 minutes, as they are already cooked down. Next, add eggs and cook, stirring regularly, until eggs are set but still slightly wet. Season with salt and pepper to taste and if you want to make it more ranchy, add some salsa. Serve with flour tortillas.

COMO DICE EL DICHO:

"DALES BASTANTE MECATE - Y SOLOS SE AHORCAN"

El Sabor De Mi Cocina

Wet Burritos

This recipe is a favorite at my Mommas' house. While we were living in the state of Michigan, mom and stepdad Domingo owned a little restaurant in which was named "PANCHO'S" after my late maternal grandfather. This was one of their top sellers. The sauce is unique and can be used for enchiladas as well. ~~Recipe compliment of Mom, Esmeralda R. Gutierrez

Ingredients:

6 Giant Size Flour tortillas (can be store bought or homemade)
1 Large bag shredded cheddar/American cheese
2 pounds ground beef or you can also use shredded chicken
4 potatoes, diced
1 onion, diced
1 green pepper (bell pepper)
½ head garlic, which is about 4-5 cloves
2 tsp ground Comino (cumin)
2 tsp ground black pepper
4 cups cooked long grain Spanish rice
1 skillet cooked and mashed homemade beans

El Sabor De Mi Cocina

Procedure:

Cook ground beef until browned. While browning process is going on, alternatively add all the spices and the onion, peppers. Cook the rice and beans on separate skillets and set aside. You will be using these to fill your burritos.

Lay tortillas, slap on a thin layer of refried beans, then add some cheese (sprinkled on to your desire), add some rice. If you don't want it too thick, just add about 2 tbsp of the cooked rice over the cheese. Then add meat, again to your liking. Some people like it more on the meat lovers' side, so they add more. Next, fold your burrito like if you were making an envelope.

Place your wrapped-up burrito on a large plate and sprinkle more cheese on top and smother it with my homemade burrito sauce to your desire. Place it in microwave or oven to melt the cheese, serve with lettuce, tomatoes sour cream and avocado on top.

For Sauce Ingredients:

½ head of garlic (which is about 4-5 cloves)
2 tsp ground Comino (cumin)
1 tsp ground black pepper
½ serving spoon
2 tsp Worcestershire sauce
½ serving spoon of Gebhart chili powder
1/2 to 1 serving spoon of flour

*Note: before you add the flour; mix it well in 1 cup of water. Dissolve it well, until you see no more clumps.

COMO DICE EL DICHO:

"NO DEJES PARA MANANA LO QUE PUEDES HACER HOY"

Liebre en Sangrita

(Jack Rabbit Stew in Blood Gravy)

Yes, you read this right. Grandma would also cook jack rabbit stew. And used its own blood for the gravy. Just like the Cabrito, in which the older generation calls it Fritada de Cabrito. So, we can say, this, is Fritada de Liebre.

Ingredients:

2 Jack Rabbits, skinned, gutted and cleaned

½ head garlic (about 4-5 cloves)

2 tsp ground Comino (Cumin)

Salt to taste

Jack Rabbit blood

Water

1 bell pepper

1/2 onion

Procedure:

When you are ready to skin your rabbits, soon as you have skinned it but have not degutted it, you first make a slit cut on its lower jaw to collect the blood in a large bowl. When you see there is no more flowing blood add about 2 tbsp of table salt and quickly mix it.

This procedure is done so that the blood does not clump and get hard. You may have to do this in 2 separate bowls as you have 2 rabbits. Then you degut the rabbits, clean them and cut them up as if you were cutting up a whole chicken into sections.

In a large skillet, add about ½ cup of vegetable oil to sauté the rabbit pieces. Next you add in the water. Just enough to cover the rabbit in the skillet. Soon after it starts to boil, add your spices, let cook down for about 15-20 minutes. Add the onion and the bell pepper; let cook again for another 15 minutes. Cooking a total time of about 40-50 minutes to 1 hour.

To make the gravy, first add about ¼ cup of flour to the boiled down meat. Stirring it enough to prevent the clumping. Next add the rabbit blood to the mixture and stir with a whisk, as you are pouring it, again to prevent the clumping. It will start to thicken slowly like gravy. Keep stirring until it has cooked another 10-15 minutes.

Serve with a side of Mexican rice and homemade flour tortillas.

COMO DICE EL DICHO:

"LO QUE NO MATA – ENGORDA"

Picadillo de Liebre

(Jack Rabbit Hash)

After a long afternoon of rabbit hunting, we could not leave the hunting grounds without a jack rabbit, for the delicious delicacy Grandma would cook. As you can read, there are several different types of recipes here on how to prepare a Jack Rabbit.

Ingredients:

2 Jack Rabbit, skinned, cleaned and degutted

4 cloves of garlic, diced and mashed

¼ cup of all-purpose flour (for gravy)

2 tsp ground Comino (Cumin powder)

Salt & pepper to taste

Gebhart chili powder

½ onion, diced

½ bell pepper sliced

Water – enough to cover the rabbit for boiling, plus extra when it is time to make the actual Hash.

Procedure:

After the jack rabbit has been cleaned and degutted, cut it up into portions so that you can bring it to a boil in a big skillet. Once it is done, debone it and cut it up into very finely chopped pieces, just like Hash. Then bring it to another skillet with a little bit of cooking oil. Just enough to sauté the Hash for about 20 minutes. While it is sauteing add the onion and the bell pepper until it is tender enough. Next add the spices and cook down another 10 minutes. If you notice that the Hash is getting too dry, add some water just enough to keep it cooking. As it comes to a dry again, sprinkle in the flour and stir it quickly so that it will mix in evenly and without big clumps. Slowly add more water to get it to a gravy consistency. It all depends on how much gravy you want your Hash to have, is the amount of more water you will add.

Once it is to your consistency liking, add chili powder to taste. Grandma would make it to where it was semi red, because as it cooks a little longer, more or less another 15 minutes, just enough to cook the chili powder, this will turn a darker red and the taste is so good.

Once again, serve it with a side of rice and perhaps some ranchero beans.

COMO DICE EL DICHO:

"MEJOR SOLO - QUE MAL ACOMPANADO"

Frijoles Rancheros

Ingredients:

1 pound of fresh pinto beans

½ cup shortening

1 onion, diced

1 bell pepper, diced

2 serrano peppers, diced

2 fresh whole tomatoes

1 fresh cilantro, about 1 cup

1 package of Chorizo (I prefer Chorizo San Manuel) but you can use whatever you like.

1 package of Franks, sliced and chopped (hot dog Franks)

Water

Procedure:

*Note: Before you start to prepare the cooking of your beans, you must clean your beans by looking through them to make sure there are no dirt rocks mixed in. Rinse them well and set them aside.

In a large pot bring to boil about 6 cups of water. Add the rinsed pintos and bring your stove temperature to a medium temperature.

After about 30 minutes of cooking, add the ½ cup shortening to help the beans cook a little faster. And just let them cook down making sure the water level stays about the same. If you notice it go down, just add another cup or so. But not too much. You want to just have enough so that the beans are soupy.

When the beans are soft and tender and their color has changed to a nice rosy brown color, add the cooked and fat drained chorizo and stir. Also add the sliced Franks and stir. If you feel the whole package of Franks is too much, then only use ½ a package. Let that cook another 15 to 20 minutes. Lastly, add the diced onion, bell pepper, serrano's, tomatoes and chopped up cilantro. Let that cook once again for another 20 minutes. Add some salt to taste.

COMO DICE EL DICHO:

"NADIE SABE LO QUE HAY EN LA HOLLA - MAS LA CUCHARA QUE LA MENEA"

Tamales

(Filling is your choice)

Tamales tostaditos en el Comal...yummy, with a side cup of café con leche in the morning for breakfast is what I remember every time Grandma would make these. Most of the time our tamales were made from wild meat. Which was pork and deer meat mixed. The pork would cut part of the wild taste out of the cooked filling. But, oh, what a delicacy. If cooked with enough and adequate spices, you could not even taste the difference.

Ingredients:

4 cups Maseca or Masa Harina

3 cups broth (beef, chicken, vegetable or plain water)

2 tsp baking powder

1 tsp salt

1-1/3 cups lard or shortening

8 oz dried corn husks

Procedure:

Place the corn husks in the sink and pour a kettle of boiling water over them, let them soak for 30 minutes until soft. Next prepare your desired fillings. It can be anything you want, pork, beef, chicken or beans & cheese. I like to add sliced jalapenos to the beans and cheese.

To make the dough (masa), in a large bowl, use your hands to work the lard until fluffy, about 5 minutes using a kneading motion. Slowly add the maseca, baking powder, salt, in a separate bowl; stir into the lard mixture and work the dough. It will be a little crumbly due to the lard.

Add the broth, little at a time to form a very soft dough. Beat on high speed for several minutes. The dough should spread like creamy peanut butter and be a little sticky. Cover the mixing bowl with a damp paper towel, to keep the dough from drying out.

Now to make your tamales, lay a corn husk, with the glossy side up, on the counter with the wide end at the top. Scoop about 1/8 to ¼ cup of dough onto the top, middle of the husk. To spread the masa into a thin layer, about ¼" thick, use a spoon or butter knife to spread it. Leave the top part of the husk without dough so that it can be folded down after you roll them up.

Then, add 1-2 tablespoons of desired filling in a line down the center of the dough. (You do not want too much filling). Next, roll the tamale carefully, making sure the filling is covered as you roll and fold the top of the husk down.

Cook on the stove-top or Instant Pot & add water to the bottom of your steamer or instant pot. (About 1 cup for pot and a few cups for a steamer pot—don't fill above the steamer rack.) Lay a few extra corn husks on the bottom rack to keep the tamales from falling through and any boiling water from directly touching them.

Place tamales standing upright, with their open end up, just tightly enough to keep them standing. If using a steamer pot, lay a few soaked corn husks or a wet towel over the top of the tamales before closing the lid.

Steamer: Bring water to a boil (in Mexico they would often place a coin at the bottom of the steamer and when the coin started to tap in the pot you know the water was boiling.) Once boiling, reduce to a simmer and steam for 45 minutes to 1 hour. Check them after 45 minutes.

In an instant pot cook on Manual/High Pressure for 25 minutes. Allow pressure to naturally release for 10 minutes, and then quick release.

Finally, test to if the tamales are done by removing one and try to pull the husk off. If the husk pulls away cleanly from the tamale, they are done. If the dough is still sticky or wet looking, cook them for 5-10 minutes longer and try again.

Store leftover tamales in the refrigerator for 5-7 days depending on the freshness of your ingredients.

Note: You will need about 4 cups of filling for one batch of tamale dough.

COMO DICE EL DICHO:

"BUENO ES EL VINO - CUANDO ES DEL FINO"

Pizza Burgers

My nephew, Isaac, loves them. They are somewhat on the sloppy joe side, but the unique pizza ingredients make them into pizza burgers.

Ingredients:

1-pound hamburger meat

½ onion, diced

1 package sliced pepperoni

1 package shredded mozzarella cheese

1 jar pizza sauce

1 tsp oregano

1 package small hamburger buns

Non-stick cooking spray

Procedure:

In a large skillet, bring to cook the hamburger meat. Drain off all the fat. Add the diced onion, oregano and cook down another 2-3 minutes.

Next add the pizza sauce, according to your judgement. Some of you may like a lot and some may like just some.

Prepare your small hamburger buns on a cookie sheet sprayed with non-stick spray. Add a serving spoon of the meat mixture, line 4 slices of pepperoni on top of the meat, top with mozzarella cheese.

Place the top part of the buns right on top of the cheese and bake in the oven for about 5 minutes, just long enough to get the cheese melted.

Serve with chips on the side.

COMO DICE EL DICHO:

"ACEITE DE OLIVA – TODA MAL QUITA"

Caldo de Pollo

(Chicken Soup)

Ingredients:

5 pounds chicken leg quarters

2 gallons water

2 tbsp minced garlic

2 tbsp salt

1 tbsp garlic powder

4 cubes chicken bouillon

4 large carrots, peeled and cut into thick slices

4 large potatoes, peeled if desired and cut into chunks

4 zucchinis, cut into large slices

1 – 2 chayote's, cut up into chunks

1 large white onion, cut up into large, diced chunks

½ bunch of fresh chopped cilantro

Procedure:

Place the chicken legs into a large kettle and pour water over the chicken legs, add garlic, salt, garlic powder & cover. Bring to a boil and reduce the heat to low. Simmer until the chicken meat is semi off bones, but not too much. About 1 hour. Stir in the chicken bouillon cubes and let dissolve.

Mix in the carrots, potatoes, zucchini, chayote and white onion in the broth. Turn heat to medium-low and cook the soup until the vegetables and potatoes are tender, about 45 minutes to an hour. Stir in chopped cilantro in the soup, simmer for another 5 minutes. Turn off and serve with a side of Mexican rice to add to your soup as you eat.

COMO DICE EL DICHO:

"A FALTA DE PAN - BUENAS SO LOAS SEMITAS"

Caldo de Res

(Beef Soup)

Ingredients:

2 pounds beef shank, with bone

1 tbsp vegetable oil

2 tsp salt

2 tsp ground black pepper

1 onion, chopped

1 can diced tomatoes (14.5 oz)

3 cups beef broth

4 cups water

2 medium carrots, sliced

¼ cup chopped fresh cilantro

2 ears corn, husks removed & cleaned, cut into 3rds

2 chayote's, cut into chunks

1 medium head cabbage, cored and cut into large chunks

¼ cup sliced jalapenos

¼ cup diced onion

1 cup fresh chopped cilantro

Procedure:

Cut the meat from the beef bones into 1/2 "pieces, leaving some meat on the bone.

Heat a large kettle over medium-high heat until hot. Add the oil, moving the kettle around to coat the bottom completely. Add the meat and bones, season with salt and pepper. Cook and stir until thoroughly browned.

Add 1 onion, cook until onion is also lightly browned. Stir in the tomatoes and broth. The liquid should cover the bones by ½ ". If not add more water to get it there. Reduce the heat to low, and simmer for 1 hour with the lid on. If the meat is not soft, continue cooking for another 10 minutes or so. Pour in the water and return to low heat. Add the carrots, ¼ cup cilantro, and cook for 10 minutes. Now add the corn and the chayote. Simmer on low-medium until the vegetables are soft and tender. Finally, add the cabbage chunks into the soup, and cook for about 15-20 more minutes to get the cabbage tendered.

Serve into large bowls & garnish with sliced jalapenos, minced onion & fresh cilantro. Squeeze lime juice to add the extra taste kick.

COMO DICE EL DICHO:

"DONDE NO AY GORDURA - NO AY HERMOSURA"

El Sabor De Mi Cocina

Migas

(Breakfast Corn Hash)

Ingredients:

7-10 corn tortillas

6 large whole eggs

Salt to taste

4 tbsp cooking oil

Procedure:

Tear the corn tortillas into 1" pieces.

Whisk the eggs to scrambled consistency. Add the salt to taste.

In a large frying skillet, add the cooking oil and wait a couple minutes for it to get hot. Then, add the tortilla pieces. And cook them to golden-brown stage. As if they were chips. Stirring continuously to prevent them from burning.

They are now ready to add the scrambled egg mixture. And cook until the egg is done, incorporating them both together.

Serve immediately and eat alone or with flour tortillas and some salsita roja.

COMO DICE EL DICHO:

"LA SORRA NUNCA SE VE LA COLA"

El Sabor De Mi Cocina

Guisado de Javelina

(Javelina Gravied Stew)

Growing up in south Texas and with my grandparents, not only taught me to be humble and honest but also to learn to eat what was available to keep the wolf back from the door. Most people are grossed out by the simple thought of eating a non-marketed piece of meat from the wild. Non the less, meat from the wild is the cleanest there can be. For they are raised on plants, wild grass and weeds. Keeping themselves hydrated by drinking from any available source, such as puddles "when" it rains. Making the meat on their bones non greasy and clean for the human body system. Or at least this is how I see it. Yes, I did eat this and will eat it again if I had to. The best way I remember eating this is when Grandpa would make the Javelina Ribs out on the pit. Just seasoned with lots of lemon pepper and corn tortillas heated on the grill as well. Praising God, I am as healthy as can be. Having eaten this did not hurt me none. Look at me today! 😊

Ingredients:

3 pounds Javelina meat cut into chunks
6 cloves of garlic – peeled, finely diced and mushed on the molcajete
1 can tomato sauce
4 tbsp vegetable oil for cooking the meat
1 small onion
½ bell pepper, sliced
2 tsp ground Comino (cumin)
4 tbsp all-purpose flour (for thickening)

Sat and pepper to taste
½ bushel of fresh cilantro, bottoms trimmed off. Cut into 3 sections before adding to cook

Procedure:

Cut the meat into chunks, rinse and set aside.

Bring a skillet to high heat and add 4 tbsp vegetable oil to sizzling consistency.

Now add the rinsed meat chunks, being cautious for the oil is hot and as the sizzling can splatter to your skin and cause burning. (be cautious)

Let meat cook ½ way, stirring continuously to prevent sticking.

Add the spices; Comino, garlic, 1 tsp salt and stir. Let cook 5 minutes.

Add whole sliced onion and bell pepper, to the mixture, stir and let cook another 10 minutes.

Next sprinkle the 4 tbsp flour into the meat mixture and stir until you see the flour turning a golden-brown color, looking a little on the toasty side.

Add 2 cups of water and stir quickly to prevent clumping of the flour. You will now see the gravy starting to look smooth. If you feel it is not watery enough, add another cup of water to get it to its consistency.

Now add the can of tomato sauce, cilantro and cook on low heat for 15 minutes or so. Just enough to notice the color of the tomato sauce has changed from light reddish to a darker shade. Done, enjoy the Guisado de Javelina.

If desired, accompany this meal with a side of rice, beans and flour tortillas.

COMO DICE EL DICHO:

"BUENO, LE DIJO LA MULA AL FRENO - HABIENDO SACATE Y AGUA, TODO ESTA BUENO"

Pachucos

(Empanadas de Carne)

Ingredients:

2 cups instant corn flour – Masa (Maseca)
1½ cups water
1 small potato (boiled & skinned)

Procedure:

Mash the potato as if to make it for mashed potatoes. Then mix the rest of the ingredients in with the mashed mixture for about 2 minutes to form a soft dough. If the dough feels dry, add more water one tablespoon at a time. Divide into 12-15 equal balls. Pat them with the palm of your hands to stretch them out to tortilla shape. Or use a tortilla press to extend them.

Then fill them lightly, add a little bit of cheese, fold over and seal the edges. And take to the frying pan for browning on both sides, let them drain off excess fat on paper towels. Serve with a side of Mexican rice, salad and a dollop of sour cream on top.

Filling:

1 pound of hamburger meat
2 large potatoes diced and cooked as if for fried potatoes.
1 tsp Comino (cumin)
1 tsp ground black pepper
Salt to taste
1 package Colby Jack cheese
Water

Procedure:

Cook the hamburger meat very well, add spices and dash of salt. Once cooked, drain off the fat and add the diced potatoes previously fried in a separate skillet. Add a little water, just enough to get the mixture wet a little to prevent it from seeping through the tortilla. If it tears the tortilla, while it is frying, you will have a mess in the skillet as it is browning. So, fill generously, but enough to form the pachuco.

COMO DICE EL DICHO:
"HECHALE MAS AGUA A LA SOPA"

Fried Venison Backstrap

(Lomo de Venado Empanizado)

Ingredients:

2 pounds backstrap cut into ¼ "thick slices

2 cups milk

¼ cup Italian dressing

2 tbsp Louisiana hot sauce

2 eggs

½ cup evaporated milk

3 cups all-purpose flour

2 tbsp salt

1 tbsp ground black pepper

3 cups vegetable oil for frying

Procedure:

Place the slices of meat into a bowl and pour the 2 cups milk, ¼ cup Italian dressing and hot sauce, in to coat as a marinate for 1 hour.

Heat the vegetable oil in a skillet until hot for deep frying.

In another bowl, whisk together the 2 eggs, ½ cup evaporated milk.

In another bowl, mix the flour, salt & pepper and set aside for coating.

Now, dip the meat slices into the flour, then into the egg/milk mixture, then back into the flour mixture. Shake off any excess flour.

Slowly drop into the sizzling hot oil and let sit in it until lightly browned around the edges, flip to brown the other side. For about 3-4 minutes each side. Remove from frying oil onto paper towel before serving to absorb all the excess oil.

COMO DICE EL DICHO:

"DE LA MAR, EL MERO – DE LA TIERRA, EL CARNERO"

Venison Chili

(Slow Cooked)

I personally like to cook chili in the slow cooker – this absorbs all the natural flavors the venison has for its own. The taste is awesome with a side of homemade corn bread.

Ingredients:

Slow Cooker

1-pound ground venison

¼ tsp salt

¼ tsp ground pepper

1 tbsp garlic powder

1 cup diced onion

1 jalapeño diced and minced

1 package chili seasoning

Water to its consistency (use your judgment)

1 (14 oz) can diced tomatoes

1 can (15 oz) pinto beans, drained

1 can (15 oz) kidney beans, drained

1 can (6 oz) tomato sauce

Sliced green onions (if desired)

Procedure:

In a skillet, on medium heat, brown the ground venison to full cook.

Drain off if any, fat drippings.

Add meat to slow cooker and the rest of the ingredients.

Stir

Set the slow cooker on low for 6 hours

Use a ladle to serve the chili in bowls, add green onions if desired. Serve with cornbread.

COMO DICE EL DICHO:

"BIEN ESTA SAN PEDRO EN ROMA - AUNQUE NO COMA"

El Sabor De Mi Cocina

Breads, Pastas, and Casseroles

Connie's Pan de Campo

Ingredients:

3 cups all-purpose flour (Gold Medal)

3 tsp baking powder

1 Tsp salt

¾ cup shortening

1½ cups buttermilk

Procedure:

Preheat oven to 400 degrees F. sift flour, baking powder & salt together.

Work in shortening into flour mixture. Add buttermilk. Knead dough until all mixture is smooth. Roll dough out ½ inch thick and place on a lightly greased round baking pan.

Or bake on a cast iron skillet over fire outdoors. Or like I mentioned, in the oven. Bake 10-12 minutes. Prick fork holes sporadically on dough to prevent bubbling as it is cooking. When baked halfway, brush with butter. Then brush again once done completely.

COMO DICE EL DICHO:

"LO QUE SIEMBRAS – COSECHAS"

Capirotada

(Mexican Bread Pudding)

Us Mexicans, during Lenten season – La Cuarezma, we feast on this dish. The reason being is that during Lent while some of us are abstaining from meat on Fridays, the cheese on here provides the extra protein our body needs. Although, this delicacy of our culture can be made anytime during our 365 days a year. There are plenty of versions to it – this, is mine.

Ingredients:

4 bolillos, sliced or you can use a loaf of sliced French bread dried out
½ cup room temperature butter
1 piloncillo cone
1 cinnamon stick
2 cups water
¾ cup chopped/minced pecans

½ cup raisins/craisins (either or)
1 cup grated Monterey Jack or cheddar cheese

Procedure:

Please note that the older the bread is the better the pudding will be.

Preheat the oven to 350 degrees F. slice the bread about ½ inch thick and lightly butter both sides of the bread.

Start layering them on a baking sheet and bake for 3-4 minutes on each side until lightly browned. Remove and set aside to cool.

For Tea:

Bring a small kettle to stove and place the sugar, cinnamon and water to boil. Stir the sugar until it has dissolved. Then lower the heat and let it simmer for 5 minutes. Do not stir. Now you can remove the cinnamon stick and let the syrup cool down.

Layering:

Next, you now layer the bread, pecans, raisins/craisins and cheese in the cake pan 9x13" and pour some of the syrup over, letting it soak u for about 5 minutes. Then, you will repeat the same steps by starting to layer the bread and the rest of the ingredients.

Make sure you let the syrup soak up 5 minutes between layers so that it remains in the bread and not at the bottom of the pan.

Now it is time to bake. So, put the pan in the preheated oven and bake the pudding for 30 minutes until golden brown and you can see that the cheese has been melted.

When done, make sure to let stand out of the oven at least 15 minutes before serving.

Serve hot or cold, drizzle with caramel, strawberry syrup or top with whipping cream.

COMO DICE EL DICHO:

"EN EL MODO DE PARTIR EL PAN -
SE CONOCE AL QUE ES TRAGON"

El Sabor De Mi Cocina

Tortillas

Ingredients:

1½ cups white wing flour (all purpose)

1 tsp salt

¾ tsp baking powder

¼ cup shortening

½ cup warm water

Procedure:

Preheat griddle to 400-425 degrees F

Combine flour, salt & baking powder; mix well.

Add shortening and incorporate with hands to form crumbly mixture. Slowly, add warm water; mix well.

Knead for about 5 minutes until dough is smooth & elastic. If dough appears sticky, add a little more flour. Cover dough with a damp cloth & let rest for 15 minutes. Divide dough into 8-12 portions. Roll out on a lightly floured surface to 1/8-inch thickness. Cook 1 ½ minutes on each side until lightly browned. Makes 8-12 tortillas.

(double/triple recipe for larger quantities)

COMO DICE EL DICHO:

"EL MUERTO Y EL ARRIMADO - A LOS TRES DIAS APESTAN"

El Sabor De Mi Cocina

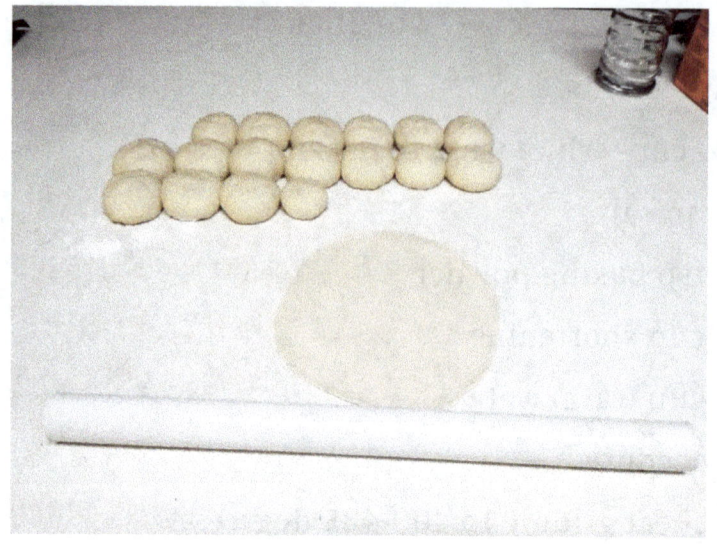

Quick Croissants

Recipe compliment of Carolina Y. Rocha - Parkman

Makes 8 Croissants

Ingredients:

2 cups strong bread flour
1¼ sticks cold unsalted butter, sliced/cubed
½ cup lukewarm whole milk
3 tbsp sugar
7 grams active dry yeast (your choice brand)
½ tsp salt

For Egg Wash:

1 - Egg yolk
1 - tbsp whole milk

Procedure:

Place yeast in a bowl. Add sugar and stir until it liquifies. Add milk and set aside to cool completely.

Combine flour and salt into a large bowl. Add butter and using a fork combine it until big crumbs form. Add the yeast/milk mixture and gently combine until the dough just comes together. The butter needs to remain in pea-sized pieces. Wrap it with plastic, knead slowly to form a square and freeze for 30 minutes or refrigerate for a couple of hours.

Dust with flour your work surface and your rolling pin. Start rolling the dough into a rectangular roughly 2-3 times as long as it is wide. The dough is hard to work with at the beginning but will come together while rolling and folding.

Fold the short sides of the dough into the middle. Rotate the dough by a quarter turn. Roll out slightly to lengthen and fold the short ends towards the middle. Flip the dough over so the seams are underneath. Repeat the rolling and folding process steps 4-5, three more times, giving the dough a total of four times of rolling and folding.

Wrap the dough in plastic wrap and refrigerate for a couple of hours or better overnight.

On a lightly floured surface roll the dough into a rectangular of 16 inches x 10 inches. Cut the dough into triangles, it will make about 8 triangles of 12 inches long and 3 inches at base.

Score a small slit in the center of each triangle base. Gently stretch the corners and tip, then roll the croissant starting from the wide up to the top giving them the croissant shape.

Place the croissants with tip side down onto a prepared baking sheet lined with parchment paper. Cover with plastic wrap and let rise 2-3 hours at room temperature.

Preheat oven to 450 degrees F. brush the croissants with egg wash.

Bake for 8 minutes then reduce the oven to 375 degrees F and bake for another 10-15 minutes until deep golden brown.

Cool on wire rack before serving.

COMO DICE EL DICHO:

"CUCHILLITO DE PALO - NO CORTA PERO BIEN QUE MAYUGA"

Sweet Corn Bread

Recipe compliment of Damiana Guerrero, Zapata, TX

Ingredients:

2 boxes Jiffy corn bread mix
2 cans cream style corn
2 eggs
1 can sweetened condensed milk

Procedure:

Mix all ingredients

Bake on a greased pan in a preheated oven to 375 degrees F for 30-45 minutes.

COMO DICE EL DICHO:
"DE TAL PALO – ESTA LA ESTILLA"

Biscuits

Ingredients:

4 cups biscuit flour or all-purpose flour
   Plus, more for dusting

4 tsp baking powder

1/2 tsp baking soda

1 Tsp salt
1 Cup unsalted butter (2 sticks cubed & very cold)
1 Cup buttermilk, plus 2 tbsp melted butter for brushing

Procedure:

Preheat oven to 375 degrees F. Line a baking sheet with parchment paper. In a large bowl, whisk together the flour, baking powder, baking soda, and salt. Using your hands or a pastry cutter, incorporate the butter into the dry ingredients, leaving large chunks.

Fold in the buttermilk until a thick dough is formed. Lightly flour a clean surface and dump the dough onto it. Bring the dough together until it comes together in one large piece.

Roll out with rolling pin to about 1 ½ -2 inches thick. Using a biscuit cutter or a small glass, cut out 2-3-inch rounds and place them on the prepared baking sheet. Its ok if biscuits are touching.

Bake for 18-20 minutes or until golden brown. Brush the biscuits with melted butter. Serve as desired. Enjoy!!

COMO DICE EL DICHO:

"CON LA VARA QUE MIDES – SERAS MEDIDO"

Shells & Tomato Sauce

Recipe compliment of Carolina Y. Rocha - Parkman

Ingredients:

3 cups shell macaroni
6 ripe tomatoes
½ cup chopped sweet white onions
¼ cup fresh chopped basil
¼ cup parsley
¼ cup olive oil
1 tsp salt
1 small clove of garlic, chopped up
¼ tsp ground black pepper

Procedure:

Remove stem ends from tomatoes. Cut into ½ inch pieces. There should be 2-2 ½ cups. Mix tomatoes, onions, basil, parsley, oil, salt, garlic & pepper in a large bowl. Set aside at room temperature. Cook shell macaroni in 4 quarts of boiling salted water until almost tender, 10-12 minutes. Drain well, add macaroni to tomatoes. Toss to blend. Serve at once.

COMO DICE EL DICHO:

"DE QUE MUEREN LOS QUEMADOS - SI NO ES DE PURO ARDOR"

El Sabor De Mi Cocina

Nina's Macaroni Casserole

Recipe compliment of Carolina Y. Rocha - Parkman

Ingredients:
1½ cup elbow macaroni
¾ lbs. Italian sausage, reg or spicy
1/3 cup chopped onion
¼ cup chopped green pepper
1 large garlic clove, chopped and diced
1/2 tsp dried oregano leaves
¼ tsp each salt & pepper
8 ounces tomato sauce (1 small can)
2 tbsp chopped parsley, this is optional
1 cup grated mozzarella cheese
½ cup parmesan cheese

Procedure:

Cook macaroni according to package directions, being careful not to overcook.

In the meantime, crumble the sausage into a large, heavy skillet.

Cook over medium heat until browned; about 10 minutes. Pour off some of the fat, leaving 1-2 tsps.

Stir in the onion, green pepper & garlic. Sauté for 5 mins until onions are soft. Add oregano, basil, salt, pepper, tomato sauce, parsley, if used & cooked macaroni. Also add in the mozzarella cheese & ¼ cup parmesan cheese. Mix well.

Spoon mixture into a 2 - quart casserole. Sprinkle with remaining parmesan cheese. Bake at 350 degrees F for 20-25 minutes until hot and golden.

COMO DICE EL DICHO:

"TODAVIA VEN LA TEMPESTAD - Y NO SE INCAN"

El Sabor De Mi Cocina

Tater Tot Casserole

Ingredients:

2 pounds ground beef
½ onion, chopped
1/8 cup Worcestershire sauce
1 tsp steak seasoning
½ tsp salt
½ tsp pepper
1 bag tater tots - 32 oz
8 ounces shredded Monterey jack cheese
8 ounces shredded cheddar cheese

Procedure:

Brown the ground beef. Add in the chopped onions & cook until soft. Stir in steak seasoning, salt, pepper & Worcestershire sauce. Place at the bottom of the greased 9x13 baking pan.

Spread out the Monterey jack cheese over the ground beef.

Place one layer of tater tots over the casserole. Bake at 375 degrees F for 25 minutes uncovered.

Sprinkle with the shredded cheese * put back in the oven until melted.

Serve immediately with your favorite burger toppings. Add more onions, tomatoes, bacon, or pickles! Whatever your heart so desires.

COMO DICE EL DICHO:

"PERRO QUE LADRA - NO MUERDE"

El Sabor De Mi Cocina

Corn Dog Batter

Ingredients:

1 cup pancake mix (not the complete mix)

½ cup yellow cornmeal

1 egg beaten

¾ cup whole milk

Procedure:

Stir together all the ingredients. Batter will be thick. Place a kabob stick about 1 inch into the frank (hot dog) then dip that into the batter. Let it drip a little so that there isn't an excess amount of batter. Fry in deep hot oil. Brown on all sides. When done, place on a paper towel to drain off excess oil.

Dip:

¾ cup ketchup

2 tbsp mustard

1/2 tsp garlic salt

Stir together, dip fried corn dog and enjoy!!

COMO DICE EL DICHO:

"AL NOPAL SOLO SE ARRIMAN CUANDO TIENE TUNAS"

El Sabor De Mi Cocina

My Daddy's Pan de Campo

*In Loving Memory of My Father
February 16, 1945 - August 1, 2020*

Ingredients:

1 - 5 lb. bag white wing ready mix flour for tortillas
¼ can of clabber girl brand baking powder
2 cans evaporated milk plus 2 cans of water
1 tub of margarine for brushing

Procedure:

Remember this is a Ready Mix so it requires no shortening

In a large mixing bowl, bring together the bag of flour, baking powder and mix to remove all the crumbles there may be.

While this is happening, bring to heat the milk and water together. Not too hot so that you can handle the kneading of the dough.

Start adding the milk mixture a little at a time to bring the dough together slowly, until it is all gathered. Next bring out to a lightly floured surface and knead, knead, knead. Leave it in the mixing bowl once worked and cover with a cloth. Dad would say, "y dejala que descanse unos 20 minutos" "let it rest about 20 minutes"

After 20 minutes are up, give it another short knead and divide the dough into 4 equal portions. Roll it out kind of chunky, prick fork holes and brush lightly with butter. Pop them in the oven one at a time for about 15 minutes on each side. When done, brush once again with butter to keep them moist and buttery.

Preheat the oven to 350 degrees F. If you notice the bread browning to fast, lower the temperature to 325 degrees F.

Serve with carne Guisada or top with shredded cheddar cheese and a nice cup of coffee to go along. That is the way, I like it.

COMO DICE EL DICHO:

"NO HAY QUE BUSCARLE RUIDO AL CHICHARRON"

Pizza Casserole

Ingredients:

1-pound ground beef or Italian sausage (or both for extra flavor)

6 ounces pepperoni

3 cups mozzarella cheese

1 28-ounce can crushed tomatoes or (2) 15-ounce cans crushed tomatoes

1 tbsp garlic salt

1 tbsp Italian seasoning

16-ounce penne pasta

¼ cup parmesan cheese

Procedure:

Preheat oven to 350 degrees F, brown the beef & drain the fat.

Pour in the crushed tomatoes, Italian seasoning & the garlic salt. Stir to combine.

Meanwhile boil pasta according to directions but cook to al dente, meaning you want the pasta to be firm & undercooked.

Drain pasta & pour half of the pasta in a 9x13 baking dish. Spoon half the meat mixture over the pasta. Top with half mozzarella cheese.

Lay half the pepperoni on top; then layer the remaining pasta, meat sauce, cheese & pepperoni.

Sprinkle the parmesan cheese on top. Cover with foil and bake for 30 minutes at 350 degrees F. remove foil & bake another 14 minutes until bubbly brown. Allow to cool 4 minutes then serve. I like to serve this with garlic bread on the side.

COMO DICE EL DICHO:

"VEN QUE EL NINO ES PEDORRO -
Y LE DAN FRIJOLES"

Easy Zucchini Bread

This recipe comes all the way from the state of Michigan. While living up there, I made a lot of friends and learned to bake and cook quite a bit of northern foods.

Ingredients:

2 cups sugar
1- cup oil
3 eggs
3 cups all-purpose flour
¼ tsp baking soda
1 tsp salt
1 tsp cinnamon (add to taste)
2 cups grated fresh zucchini
1 cup nuts, walnuts or pecans (your choice)
2 tsp vanilla

Procedure:

Mix all ingredients together – in order!!

Pour into a greased loaf pan and bake at 350 degrees F for 50 minutes or until a wooden pick inserted comes out clean.

If you want, you can also bake in a cupcake pan as if they were muffins.

COMO DICE EL DICHO:

"EL QUE NACE PA TAMAL –
DEL CIELO LE CAEN LAS OJAS"

El Sabor De Mi Cocina

Native American Fry Bread

While working at the local nursing home in Hart, Michigan I learned to make this bread. It is so soft and delicious, while its ingredients are few.

Ingredients:

3 cups all-purpose flour
6 tsp baking powder
1 tsp sugar
1 tsp salt
½ cup whole milk

Procedure:

Mix everything in a bowl until it forms a soft dough. Let sit for about an hour. Break off pieces, pat down slightly to form circles, making a small hole in the middle of the dough. Fry in hot oil (shortening or lard works too) until brown. Turn and brown the other side. Drain on paper towels. I prefer to shake mine in a bag of sugar or cinnamon/sugar and use it as a treat rather than bread.

*Note: This can also be used as the shell for the Navajo tacos or the Navajo burger buns.

COMO DICE EL DICHO:

"GUAJOLOTE QUE SALE DEL CORRAL -
TERMINA EN MOLE"

Navajo Fry Bread

This is a second version of the Fry Bread. Like I mentioned earlier, we lived in the state of Michigan for several years and while up there, I got to share time with several Native American ladies. In the little town that we lived in, after every county fair, the Navajo Indians would hold their annual Pow Wow. There I always had a feast trying out all the different booths with all sorts of Navajo dishes. The Fry Bread has always been my most favorite.

Ingredients:

6 cups unsifted all-purpose flour

1 tbsp salt

2 tbsp baking powder

½ cup instant non-fat dry milk

Lukewarm water

Lard or shortening

Procedure:

In a bowl combine flour, salt, baking powder and non-fat dry milk. Add just enough lukewarm water (about 2 3/4 cups) to make a soft dough. Knead thoroughly and pinch off a ball of dough about the size of a large egg. Shape it round and flat with a small hole in the middle, then work it back & forth from one hand to the other to make it thinner and thinner. Gradually stretching it to a diameter of about 9 inches.

Navajos slap the dough back and forth between the hands in much way Mexicans make corn tortillas. If in a hurry, you can roll out the dough like a pie crust.

In a frying pan, have ready hot fat at least an inch deep. Drop the thin round of dough into the hot fat and fry to a light brown on one side; then turn and fry on the other side. As it fry's, the bread puffs and becomes light and crisp. Drain each piece on a paper towel. Serve hot with lots of butter, jam or honey. Makes about 18-24 pieces each about the size of a 9-inch plate.

Note: This is the same bread used for the Navajo Tacos and the Navajo Burgers

COMO DICE EL DICHO:

"PARA TODO MAL MEZCAL – PARA TODO BIEN TAMBIEN"

Pineapple Zucchini Bread

Ingredients:

3 whole eggs

1 cup vegetable oil

2 cups sugar

2 tsp vanilla

2 cups shredded zucchini

3 cups all-purpose flour

2 tsp baking soda

½ tsp salt

¼ tsp baking powder

1 can 8 oz crushed pineapple, drained

1 ½ tsp ground cinnamon

1 cup chopped nuts or pecans

Procedure:

Beat eggs, oil, sugar, vanilla until thick. Stir in remaining ingredients. Blend well. Pour into 2 greased and floured loaf pans, 9x5" bake @ 350 degrees F. use a toothpick to test center after 40 minutes of baking. When dry and clean; it is done.

COMO DICE EL DICHO:
"NO SE PUEDE CHIFLAR Y COMER PINOLE
AL MISMO TIEMPO"

Apple Bread

Ingredients:

½ cup shortening
1 cup sugar
2 whole eggs
1 tsp baking soda (in 2 tbsp sour milk)
2 cups all-purpose flour
1 tsp vanilla
2 cups chopped apples, peeled and cored

Procedure:

Cream shortening & sugar. Add eggs and mix well. Add milk, flour and vanilla. Mix again. Stir in chopped apples and give them a gentle mix.

Topping:

1 tbsp melted margarine
2 tbsp flour
2 tbsp sugar
1 tsp ground cinnamon

Procedure:

Mix all until crumbly and sprinkle on top. Just like if you were making an apple crisp topping. Bake @ 350 degrees F until toothpick inserted in center comes out clean. Usually I test it at about 30 minutes. Can go up to 40 minutes, all depending on your ovens.

COMO DICE EL DICHO:
"EL MUERTO AL POZO - Y EL VIVO AL GOZO"

El Sabor De Mi Cocina

Best Banana Cake

Ingredients:

1 yellow cake mix

2 whole eggs

1 stick salted butter (1/2 cup melted)

5 ripened bananas

Procedure:

Pour cake mix in a large mixing bowl. Add 2 eggs, 1 stick melted butter, & mix with mixer. Add mased bananas & slightly incorporate into the cake batter.

Bake @ 350 degrees F for 45 minutes.

COMO DICE EL DICHO:

"DIME CON QUIEN ANDAS - Y TE DIRE QUIEN ERES"

Bunuelos Batter

(Para Molde – For Mold)

Ingredients:

1 cup all-purpose flour

1 cup warm whole milk

1 whole egg

1 pinch of salt

1 tsp vanilla

Procedure:

Mix all ingredients together with whisk. Use very hot cooking oil for frying. Slowly dip mold into batter just to edge of rim making sure the mixtures don't go over the edges to prevent it from sticking. This way it will be easier to release off the mold. Drain on paper towel. Dust in cinnamon sugar or powdered sugar and or glaze with your favorite toppings.

COMO DICE EL DICHO:

"EL QUE MUCHO SE DESPIDE –POCAS GANAS TIENE DE IRSE"

Grandma's Good Ole' Fruitcake

On occasion, Grandma used to make this. I do not know where she got the recipe from but, I do know that it was and still is to this day so delicious. The best part of this fruitcake is a glass of all-time EGG NOG with it!

Ingredients:

1 tsp baking soda
1 cup sour cream
1 cup chopped up dates (datiles)
2 cups raisins
½ cup dried sweetened cranberries
½ cup glazed cherries cut in halves
1 cup chopped walnuts/pecans
2 cups all-purpose flour
(divided into ¼ cup & 1-3/4 cups)
1 stick butter
1 cup sugar
1 large egg @ room temperature
1 tsp salt

Procedure:

Preheat the oven and prepare your loaf pans. Oven needs to be at 325 degrees F. in a 9x5" loaf pan, well-greased is where you will bake these babies 😊

Mix the sour cream and baking soda in a small bowl and set aside.

Bring together in a separate bowl the dates, raisin, cherries, cranberries and nuts with the ¼ cup of flour. Making sure, all the fruits are covered in the flour. Set this aside too.

For the batter:

Beat together butter and sugar until fluffy. Mix in the egg, sour cream and baking soda mix.

Add the flour and the salt and mix together. Combine the fruit/nut mixture with the creamed ingredients and mix well to distribute the fruits and nuts evenly.

Pour the batter into the cake loaf pans and bake in preheated oven. Note: place a separate pan of water in the oven on rack underneath where the baking pans are. This will help keep moisture to the cakes.

Bake at 325 degrees for 1-1/2 to 2 hours or until a wooden stick comes out clean.

*Keep in mind, the water pan may have to be refilled during the baking process.

Let cool out of pans completely. When ready to store, wrap well with saran wrap and then with aluminum foil.

COMO DICE EL DICHO:

"COMER SIN APETITO HACE DANIO –
Y AQUI ES DELITO"

My Momma's Pan de Campo

Ingredients:
4 cups all-purpose flour
1 tbsp salt
4 tbsp sugar
2 tsp baking powder
2 cups whole milk

Procedure:
In a large bowl mix all the dry ingredients together and add the milk. Mix to form the dough. Turn dough onto a floured surface and knead for about 3 to 4 minutes, until it is smooth.

Cut into 3 pieces and roll out into rounds about ½ "thick. Place them on a greased cast iron skillet and bake in a preheated oven at 400 degrees F for 20 to 25 minutes.

COMO DICE EL DICHO: "QUIEN HOY NO TE VALORA, MANANA TE EXTRANARA"

El Sabor De Mi Cocina

Pan De Elote Esponjoso

Ingredients:

2½ cups frozen sweet whole kernel corn

½ cup vegetable oil

1 cup all-purpose flour, sifted

1 cup sugar

1 tbsp baking powder

½ cup whole milk

4 whole eggs

2 tsp vanilla

Procedure:

Preheat oven to 350 degrees F

In a blender, add all ingredients as noted above. Blend on high speed until all are well blended & mixture is creamy. Grease a loaf pan all around and pour batter from blender into it. Bake for about 30-40 minutes or until toothpick inserted in center comes out clean & dry.

COMO DICE EL DICHO:

"DEL DICHO AL HECHO HAY MUCHO TRECHO"

El Sabor De Mi Cocina

Tuna Noodle Casserole

Ingredients:

1 package egg noodles
8 frozen veggies (1/2 a bag)
3 tbsp butter
3 tbsp all-purpose flour
1 cup chicken broth
½ cup white wine (suggestion: Chardonnay)
1 cup fat free milk
½ cup heavy cream
½ tsp poultry seasoning
Salt & pepper to taste
2 cans white albacore tuna in water, drained
¾ cup grated parmesan cheese
1 cup plain ruffles chips, crushed

Procedure:

Bring a large pot of salted water to boil. Cook egg noodles according to the package directions until Al Dente. Drain and rinse with cold water, set aside.

Replace hot pot back to medium heat. Melt butter, then whisk in flour. Cook for 1 minute. Slowly whisk in chicken stock and wine. Sauce should form & start to thicken, simmer for 3 minutes to cook out alcohol in wine.

Continue whisking to avoid getting lumps. Stir in milk, cream, poultry seasoning, salt & pepper. Cook on medium low heat for another 3 minutes. Stir in cooked noodles & veggies. Add in tuna & parmesan cheese. Stir once again. Top with crushed chips & serve.

COMO DICE EL DICHO:

"EL QUE NUNCA HA TENIDO – CUANDO LLEGA A TENER, HASTA LOCO SE QUIERE VOLVER"

Cherry Bread

Ingredients:

For Bread

¾ cup granulated sugar
½ cup whole milk
½ cup vegetable oil
1 large whole egg
1 tsp vanilla or almond extract
2 cups all-purpose flour
2 tsp baking powder
¼ tsp salt
2 jars maraschino cherries, 10 oz each

For Glaze
2 cups powdered sugar
2 tbsp melted butter
1/3 cup maraschino cherry juice
½ tsp almond extract

Procedure:

For Bread

Preheat oven to 350 degrees F. in a medium bowl, stir together sugar, milk, oil, egg & vanilla. In a separate bowl, combine the flour, baking powder & salt. Add the dry ingredients to the wet ingredients and stir until just combined.

Drain the maraschino cherries reserving the juice for the glaze. Coarsely chop the cherries in a food processor or with a knife. Gently fold the cherries into the batter. Pour the bread batter into a greased 9x5 inch bread pan and bake at 350 degrees F for 50-55 minutes. A toothpick inserted in the center of the bread should come out clean. Allow the bread to cool for 10 minutes, then remove the bread to a wire rack to cool completely.

For Glaze

Combine powdered sugar, melted butter, cherry juice & almond extract in a small bowl. Mix until it is smooth. Once the bread is cool, spread the glaze on top of the bread. Slice and serve. Freezes well.

COMO DICE EL DICHO:

"LAS PALABRAS SE LAS LLEBA EL VIENTO – Y A LAS PERSONAS EL TIEMPO"

El Sabor De Mi Cocina

Desserts

Pies, Cakes, and Cookies

Connie's Pan de Polvo

Ingredients:

3 pounds Crisco shortening
5 pounds White Wing or Gold Medal all-purpose flour
1 cup sugar

For tea:
3 to 4 cups water for tea
2 tsp anise seed
4 cinnamon sticks
1 cup cinnamon/anise tea
For dusting:
6 cups of sugar
½ cup of powdered cinnamon
(more or less – just until you see some cinnamon color in the sugar)

El Sabor De Mi Cocina

Procedure:

Cream Crisco on medium - high speed until extra creamy & fluffy. Gradually & alternatively add flour, sugar & tea; repetitively until all is gone. Note: sugar & tea will finish first while you are still adding the flour. Knead mixture in big mixing bowl as well as Crisco in between additions. Once all flour is added, continue kneading the dough in the bowl. Then divide into 6 balls and spread or roll out with a sheet of wax paper on top. For this you will have to use a rolling pin to spread it out. Or you can also hand roll with the palms of your hands to about 1/8 - ¼ inch thick.

Lift up with a metal spatula after you have pressed the cookie cutters in the dough for your design.

Dough is a little tough to pick up since it is so soft.

Note: there is no need to grease the cookie sheets. Just wipe clean with a dry cloth or paper towel after each bake.

Bake @ 350 degrees F for about 10 - 15 minutes or until you see the bottoms browned but not too brown.

Then dust in a mixture of sugar & cinnamon powder mixed. Place GENTLY in a container. You can pile them up but do not be too rough on them. They will break quite easy.

COMO DICE EL DICHO:

"PANSA LLENA - CORAZON CONTENTO"

Lady Fingers

(Deditos de Novia or Snowballs)

Ingredients:

1 cup butter, at room temperature

½ cup powdered sugar

2 tsp vanilla

2 cups all-purpose flour

¼ tsp salt

1 cup finely chopped pecans

Powdered sugar

Procedure:

Combine the softened room temperature butter with the ½ cup powdered sugar and vanilla.

Mix in the salt, flour and chopped pecans.

Form the dough in between your fingers and the palms of your hand, to kind of resemble finger like shapes. Or you can form 1" balls and place them on an ungreased cookie sheet.

Bake in a preheated oven at 325-degree F oven for 20 minutes. Just enough to see the bottoms of the cookies brownish. Let cool on a wire rack for 5 minutes and roll in powdered sugar. When cooled a little more, re roll again in the powdered sugar to coat any imperfection that did not cover the first time.

COMO DICE EL DICHO:

"BAJO UNA MALA CAPA - SE ESCONDE UN BUEN SUJETO"

Banana Nut Quick Bread

Ingredients:

Crisco nonstick cooking spray

2 cups all-purpose flour

1 tsp baking soda

¾ tsp salt

1 cup sugar

½ cup butter, softened

2 whole eggs

1 cup mashed ripe banana

1/3 cup whole milk

1 tsp vanilla

½ cup chopped walnuts or pecans

Procedure:

Heat oven to 350 degrees F. grease an 8x4 inch loaf pan with nonstick cooking spray. Stir flour, baking soda and salt in medium bowl until blended. Beat sugar and butter in large bowl with mixer on medium speed until fluffy. Beat in eggs, blend in the banana, milk and vanilla. Beat in flour mixture just until it is well blended. Sir in the walnuts. Spread it evenly in the prepared loaf pans. Bake 55 to 60 minutes or until the toothpick inserted in the center comes out clean. Cool for 5 minutes then remove from the pan to the wire rack to cool completely.

This makes 1 loaf. If you want extras just double or triple the recipe etc.

COMO DICE EL DICHO:

"CAMARON QUE SE DUERME – SE LO LLEVA LA CORRIENTE"

Galletas de Maizena

Cornstarch Cookies

A great friend of mine from Leon, Guanajuato passed on this recipe to me about 15 years ago. Let me tell you I had to translate it to English, therefore I just kept the grams in the ingredients. I keep in contact with her through social media, as she has returned to her native country.

Ingredients:

350 grams Maizena (flavored is optional)
200 grams sweetened condensed milk
125 grams unsalted butter
1 large whole egg
40 grams powdered sugar

Note: make sure all these ingredients are at room temperature

Procedure:

Put butter and powdered sugar in mixer bowl & mix thoroughly on medium speed, to a creamy consistency. Next add sweetened condensed milk and mix well until completely blended. Now add the egg yolk & blend once again. Once blended, add the Maizena (before adding it, sift it) & blend on low speed until all is blended.

Dough will be the consistency of such as if making tortillas. Once all blended, bring to a board and knead until a ball is firm and formed.

*test dough by pressing 2 fingers gently on it; there should not be nothing on your fingers from the indentation.

Now wrap kneaded dough with seran wrap & chill in the refrigerator for about 1 to 2 hours. Then remove and it is ready to work.

Finally, prepare your cookie sheet with parchment paper for best result.

Are you ready to make cookies? She would tell me. Lista para hacer tus galletitas? Me preguntaba.

Now start forming small balls by rolling them between your hands' palms & place them ½ inch apart.

Once all the cookie rounds are formed and on the cookie sheet, get a Maizena dusted fork and gently press onto the rounds to make the dough. (Just like if you were making peanut butter cookies) The fork dusting is to prevent the dough from sticking to it.

Preheat oven to 325 degrees F and bake for about 15 minutes.

Let stand about 5 minutes before transferring to a wire rack for complete cooling.

These delights will melt in your mouth.

COMO DICE EL DICHO:

"EL QUE MUCHO ABARCA - POCO APRIETA"

El Sabor De Mi Cocina

Pan de Elote

Facil – Easy

Ingredients:

4 elotes desgranados (no de lata)

4 fresh de kernelled corns (not from a can)

4 huevos enteros

4 whole eggs

1 barra de mantequilla (90g)

1 stick of butter (90g)

4 cucharas soperas de harina de trigo

4 tbsp wheat flour

1 cucharita de polvo para hornear

1 tsp baking powder

1 lata de lechera (lata de leche condensada Nestle)

1 can sweetened condensed milk (Nestle Brand)

1 2 cucharitas de vainilla

1 2 tsp vanilla

¼ taza de leche solo para ayudar a moler en la liquadora.

¼ cup of whole milk, just to help this blend in the blender.

Instrucciones:

Todos los ingredients se liquan en la liquadora hasta integrar. Se vacian en un molde engrasado y harinado. Se hornea a 180 grados por 40 minutos, hasta que al introducer un palillo y este salga limpio.

Procedure:

All the ingredients are to be blended in a blender until all is pureed. Pour into a greased & floured pan. Bake at 350 degrees F for 40 minutes or until a toothpick inserted comes out clean and free of crumbs.

*Rosea con miel de abeja al gusto al servir (opcional)

*drizzle with honey at serving (optional)

COMO DICE EL DICHO:

"A LA MESA Y A LA CAMA - SOLO UNA VES SE LLAMA"

El Sabor De Mi Cocina

Lemonade Pie

Ingredients:

1 (6) oz can frozen lemonade

1 14 oz can sweetened condensed milk

1 (8) oz container of cool whip or whipped cream

1 graham cracker crust (I buy this already made)

Procedure:

In a medium bowl, using a handheld mixer, mix all ingredients above until fluffy. (except for crust – of course)

Next pour into ready made crust. Refrigerate until firm, usually let set over night or at least 4 hours. This pie can also be made with limeade.

Topping: whipped cream (can) to your liking.

COMO DICE EL DICHO:

"CON PAN Y VINO SE ANDA EL CAMINO"

Easy Cheesecake

Ingredients:

1 (8) oz cream cheese; softened

1 can sweetened condensed milk (14oz)

½ cup lemon juice

1 tsp vanilla

1 graham cracker pie crust (I purchase mine already made)

1 can pie filling; cherry, strawberry etc. (your choice)

Procedure:

Beat cream cheese until smooth. Gradually mix in sweetened condensed milk, beating until smooth. Stir in the lemon juice and vanilla. Pour into the crust and refrigerate until firm. Top with pie filling of your choice. Cover tightly and refrigerate. Serves 6-8

COMO DICE EL DICHO:

"CON PERMISO DIJO ROMALDO - Y SE TOMO EL CALDO"

Pan de 5 Tazas

This recipe only calls for 1 cup of the 5 main ingredients. I use this for many things. When I make an upside-down pineapple cake or just any cake, I use this. It has the texture of a pound cake. In the long run it is very quick and simple to make.

Ingredients:

1 cup all-purpose flour

1 cup pancake mix (not the complete)

1 cup sugar

1 cup vegetable oil

1 cup whole milk

1 tsp vanilla

1 tsp baking powder

3 whole eggs

Procedure:

Bring the first 5 ingredients together in a large mixing bowl. Mix them in using a whisk so that the ingredients are lump free.

Pour into a greased and floured cake pan. Makes a great 9x13" cake. Bake in a preheated oven at 350 degrees F for about 30 - 40 minutes or until a wooden pick comes out clean and dry.

You can also put frosting of your choice on this cake or eat it just as if it was a plain pound cake.

COMO DICE EL DICHO:

"CON LA BARRIGA LLENA - SE PIENSA MEJOR"

Bunuelos

(Traditionally my Version)

Ingredients:

1 large egg, well beaten

½ cup whole milk

2 tbsp butter, melted

2 cups white wing all-purpose flour

El Sabor De Mi Cocina

¾ tsp baking powder

½ tsp salt

2 tbsp sugar

Vegetable oil for frying

Cinnamon & sugar mixture for dusting

Procedure:

Preheat oil to 375 degrees F. In a large bowl, combine egg, milk & butter, blend well. Add white wing flour, baking powder, salt & sugar. Mix well, turn onto a lightly floured surface & knead gently (3 to 5 minutes) until dough is smooth & elastic, divide into 12 balls. Roll out to 6-inch circles. Fry in deep, hot oil until lightly browned on both sides. Drain on paper towel, sprinkle with cinnamon & sugar mixture.

Makes 12 Bunuelos

*Note: if you want to add a touch of spark to these great tasting delicacies; add some fruit, pie filling and cool whip then drizzle with chocolate or caramel syrup. It is to fall over for!

COMO DICE EL DICHO:

"CON AZUCAR Y MIEL – HASTA LOS CARACOLES SABEN BIEN"

Lemon Brownies

Recipe compliment of Carolina Y. Rocha - Parkman, Friendswood, TX

Ingredients:

For brownies
1 cup unsalted butter, softened
1½ cups sugar
2 tbsp lemon zest
4 large eggs
2 tbsp fresh lemon juice
1½ cups all-purpose flour
1 tsp baking powder (for lemon glaze)
1½ cups powdered sugar
3 tbsp fresh lemon juice
3 tbsp lemon zest

Procedure:

Preheat oven to 350 degrees F & line a 9x13' baking pan with parchment paper. Using a large bowl, whisk together the flour & baking powder. Using a standing mixer, beat together the butter, sugar, lemon juice & lemon zest until light & fluffy. Beat in eggs, one at a time until combined, pour batter into the baking pan & bake in the oven for 25-28 minutes or until a toothpick comes out with moist crumbs. Make sure to not over bake. Allow to completely cool on the counter. Using a large mixing bowl, whisk together the powdered sugar, lemon juice & lemon zest until combined. Pour the glaze over the lemon bars & spread evenly. Allow to harden overnight before enjoying.

COMO DICE EL DICHO:

"CUAL ES LA FRUTA QUE DA MIEDO?
EL COOOOCOOOO"

Coconut Cream Pie Cake

Recipe compliment of Carolina Y. Rocha - Parkman Friendswood, TX

Ingredients:

1 box yellow cake mix

1 can coconut milk or cream

1 can sweetened condensed milk

8 oz cool whip

1 small package sweetened flaked coconut

Procedure:

Make the yellow cake according to package directions & bake in a 9x13" baking pan or dish. While baking the cake, mix one can of coconut cream or milk with a can of sweetened condensed milk. You can use any brand; I personally pick it up at the dollar store as it costs less.

When the cake is done & while it is still hot, take a skewer or a chop stick & poke holes evenly all the way through the cake. Be sure to poke holes along the sides of the cake if possible. Leave the cake in the pan or dish by the way. Pour the coconut milk/condensed milk over the cake evenly until it is all used. It will pool along the cake but that is ok. Let the cake cool in the pan or dish then put it in the refrigerator. When the cake is cold, spread the cool whip over the cake and sprinkle the flaked coconut over the top. If you can, make these one or two days ahead of time. The consistency is like a coconut cream pie.

COMO DICE EL DICHO:

"CUANDO EL HAMBRE ENTRA POR LA PUERTA, EL AMOR SALE POR LA VENTANA"

Easy as 1-2-3 Peanut Butter Fudge

I love to share my sweets when I make them. This recipe is so simple and quick. Like, literally quick. Plus, the ingredients may already be in your pantry at home. As I mentioned, I like to share my baked goodies. I have a customer in Freer, TX where I work that loves this fudge. I usually always make him his own 8x8" pan. His wife tells me that, he does not like to share it so, he eats it all by himself.

Ingredients:

1 can vanilla frosting

1 (18 oz) creamy or crunchy peanut butter

Procedure:

Remove the lid off the can of frosting, place it in the microwave for 10 seconds, stir it if soft enough to. Put back in the microwave for another 10 seconds and stir once again. Once it is completely melted and runny, pour it over the peanut butter. But make sure the peanut butter is already taken out of the jar and into a bowl.

Quickly stir it and once mixed, pour it into an 8x8" pan and just let it set until the fudge starts to firm. Let cool completely then refrigerate covered with seran wrap. Cut into 2x2" squares and enjoy!

COMO DICE EL DICHO:

"TIN MARIN, DE DOS PINGUE, CUCARA MACARA TITERE FUE – YO NO FUI, FUE TETE, PEGALE, PEGALE QUE ELLA MERITA FUE"

El Sabor De Mi Cocina

Frozen Pudding Pops

Ingredients:

4 oz package instant chocolate pudding mix OR your favorite flavor

2 cups whole milk

Procedure:

In a mixing bowl, combine the ingredients. Pour mixture into small plastic cups, or ice molds if you have them, and place in the freezer.

When set, but not completely frozen, you need to check about 5 to 10 minutes once they have been in the freezer. Place a wooden craft spoon into them. Serve when frozen.

COMO DICE EL DICHO:

"CUANDO EL RATON ESTA LLENO - HASTA LA HARINA LE SABE AMARGA"

El Sabor De Mi Cocina

Teacup Cookies

Recipe compliment, Carolina Y. Rocha - Parkman
Friendswood, TX

Ingredients:

1 cup butter or margarine
½ cup powdered sugar
1½ tsp vanilla
2 cups all-purpose flour
Dash of salt
Dash of baking powder
¾ cup finely chopped pecans
Powdered sugar, for dusting

Procedure:

In a bowl, beat together the butter & the powdered sugar until smooth & creamy. Add the vanilla and blend together flour, salt & baking powder. Note: just a dash

Add flour mixture to butter mixture, blending well. Add the chopped nuts, combine well. Roll the dough out into two balls. Wrap in plastic wrap & chill for at least 1 hour in the fridge. Flatten dough out & cut into 15 to 16 equal size pieces.

Shape into small marble-sized balls. Place on ungreased cookie sheets.

Bake at 375 - 400 degrees F for 10 to 12 minutes each sheet until firm but not brown. While still warm, roll or dust with powdered sugar.
Let cool, roll again in powdered sugar.

COMO DICE EL DICHO:
"CUANDO LA BURRA ES MANIOSA - AUNQUE LA CARGUEN DE SANTOS"

El Sabor De Mi Cocina

Grandpa Cowboy Cookies

Ingredients:

1 cup sifted all-purpose flour
½ tsp baking soda
¼ tsp baking powder
¼ tsp salt
¼ pound sweet butter
½ tsp vanilla
½ cup sugar
½ cup firmly packed dark brown sugar
1 large egg
1 cup quick cooking rolled or regular oats (not instant)
½ cup semi sweet mini chocolate chips
½ cup walnuts or pecans broken into medium sized pieces.

Procedure:

Position 2 oven racks to divide the oven into 3rds, preheat oven to 350 degrees F and line cookie sheets with foil. Sift together the flour, baking soda, baking powder, and salt; set aside. In a big bowl, cream the butter, add in the vanilla & both sugars, beat well. Add in egg & beat well. On low speed, gradually add the dry ingredients and beat scaping the bowl with a rubber spatula, until well blended.

Remove bowl from mixer, stir in oats & then chocolate chips, nuts. Dough will be kind of stiff. Use a well-rounded teaspoonful of the dough to make each cookie. Place the mounds 2 inches apart on the foil. Bake for about 18 minutes until cookies are golden and completely dry. Transfer to cookie rack for cooling.

COMO DICE EL DICHO:

"CUANDO EL RIO SUENA - ES PORQUE AGUA LLEVA"

Simple Pineapple Cake

*NOTE: There is no oil or butter in this cake!

Ingredients:

2 cups all-purpose flour

2 cups sugar

2 whole eggs

1 tsp baking soda

1 tsp vanilla

Pinch of salt

1 can (20 oz) crushed pineapple (undrained)
   In its own juice -not syrup

1 cup chopped nuts, optional

Cream cheese frosting:

½ cup butter or 1 stick

8 oz cream cheese, softened

1 tsp vanilla

1 ½ cup powdered sugar

Procedure:

Preheat oven to 350 degrees F. Mix all cake ingredients together in a bowl. Pour into a 9x13" greased pan, bake at 350 degrees F for 35 to 40 minutes, until the top is golden brown.

Frosting:

Beat butter, cream cheese, vanilla together until creamy. Gradually add & mix in the powdered sugar until well blended. Next frost cake with cream cheese frosting while still somewhat warm. Sprinkle with chopped nuts if desired.

COMO DICE EL DICHO:

"LO QUE NO PUEDES VER – EN TU CASA LO HAS DE TENER"

Three Ingredient Peanut Butter Cookies

Ingredients:

1 cup creamy peanut butter

1 cup sugar (regular or brown)

1 whole egg

Procedure:

Place ingredients in a medium bowl & mix to combine.

It will be soft, too soft for scooping. Refrigerate 10 minutes. Meanwhile, preheat oven to 350 degrees F. Place 1 tbsp scoops of cookie dough onto cookie sheet about 2 inches apart.

Dip a fork in a bowl of hot tap water (this stops fork from sticking to dough). Press down on dough, then press 90 degree the other way, criscross so that the cookie is shaped. Bake 10 minutes or until the surface & edges are golden brown. Or longer if you want a crunchier cookie. Let cool on a tray. Store in an airtight container. Lasts up to 4-5 days.

COMO DICE EL DICHO:

"CUANDO NO TE TOCA AUNQUE TE PONGAS – CUANDO TE TOCA AUNQUE TE QUITES"

My Decca Doll Cake

The Decca Doll, who is she? A music label from the early 60's that nicknamed an American country music legend after she skyrocketed a music single to the top, on the music charts. Non the less, my #1 admiration.

Ingredients:

1 box German chocolate cake mix
1 can sweetened condensed milk
1 cup cool whip
3 snickers bars, frozen
1 jar caramel topping

Procedure:

Prepare & bake cake according to package directions using a 9x13" cake pan. While warm, poke holes halfway into cake about 1 inch apart. Pour sweetened condensed milk over entire cake covering the holes poked. Pour caramel topping over cake & refrigerate.

When cool, top with cool whip and crushed Snickers candy. Refrigerate overnight before serving.

COMO DICE EL DICHO:

"CUATRO PLATILLOS TIENE EL POBLANO - PUERCO, COCHINO, CERDO Y MARRANO"

Pan de Elote

If you have read this book line per line, then you have probably noticed that this is the 3rd version of this recipe. For one, it is one of my all-time favorite desserts. Secondly, there are several versions to it. It just depends on which one will work for you. This is the one I use most of the time. It is all mixed in a blender, therefore, it is so quick and easy to prepare.

Ingredients:

Blender

1¼ cup yellow kernel corn (raw)
6 whole eggs
1¼ cup white kernel corn (raw)
2 cups sweetened condensed milk
½ cup cream cheese
¼ cup vegetable oil
1 tsp baking powder
2½ cups all-purpose flour (sifted)

Procedure:

Place all ingredients in blender in order as stated above. Blend for 3-4 minutes until all blended. Pour into a greased and floured or only plain heavily greased 8x10" rounded cake pan. Bake in a preheated oven at 350 degrees F for 45 minutes.

When toothpick comes out clean after inserted in center, it is then done. Let cool & flip over to a serving plate. Drizzle with your favorite topping & cool whip if desired. I like to drizzle with cajeta Mexicana or caramel.

COMO DICE EL DICHO:

"CUANDO TE SIENTES A COMER – LOS CODOS EN LA MESA, NO HAS DE PONER"

Snow White Cake

Ingredients:

2 cups flour

2 tsp baking powder

½ tsp salt

½ cup shortening

2 whole eggs

1½ cup sugar

1 tsp vanilla

1¼ cup whole milk

Procedure:

Preheat oven to 350 degrees F

Mix shortening, eggs, sugar, vanilla & milk. Then add dry ingredients together to the mixture. Pour into a well-greased 9x12" pan.

Bake at 350 degrees F for 40 minutes or until center picked with a toothpick comes out clean.

Frost with your favorite kind of frosting.

COMO DICE EL DICHO:

"COME Y BEBE – QUE LA VIDA ES BREVE"

El Sabor De Mi Cocina

Cream Cheese Frosting

Ingredients:

½ cup butter

1 (8) oz package cream cheese

1-pound powdered sugar

1 tsp vanilla

Procedure:

Combine butter, cream cheese & vanilla in a bowl, beat until smooth.

Gradually, add powdered sugar beating very well.

If mixture is too thick, add a little bit of milk & beat a little more until smooth.

COMO DICE EL DICHO:

"COMER BIEN PARA VIVIR MEJOR"

El Sabor De Mi Cocina

Hot Milk Cake

Ingredients:

4 eggs
2 cups sugar
1 tsp vanilla
2¼ cups all-purpose flour
2¼ tsp baking powder
1¼ cup 2% milk
10 tbsp butter, cubed

Procedure:

In a large bowl, beat eggs on high speed for 5 minutes or until thick & lemon colored. Gradually, add sugar, beating until mixture is light & fluffy. Beat in vanilla. Combine flour & baking powder; gradually add to batter, beat at low speed until smooth.

In a small saucepan, beat milk & butter just until butter is melted. Gradually add to batter, beat just until combined.

Pour into a greased 9x13" baking pan. Bake at 350 degrees F for 30-35 minutes or until a toothpick inserted near center comes out clean. Cool on a wire rack.

Top with cool whip & strawberries, raspberries or blueberries.

COMO DICE EL DICHO:
"COMER SIN APETITO ACE DANIO Y ES DELITO"

Connie's Oatmeal White Chocolate Craisin Cookies

I am a lover of all things White Chocolate. Better yet, White Almond Bark. As Candy, one of my co-workers say, "Connie, chocolate is chocolate. There is no such thing as White Chocolate." This cookie combination is my favorite. I have no limit.

2/3 cup butter or margarine, softened
2/3 cup brown sugar
2 large eggs
1½ cup old fashioned oats
1½ cups flour
1 tsp baking soda
1 tsp salt
15 oz package craisins
2/3 cup white chocolate chips

Procedure:
Preheat oven to 375 degrees F, using an electric mixer, beat butter or margarine & sugar together in a medium mixing bowl until light & fluffy. Add eggs mixing well. Combine oats, flour, baking soda & salt in a separate mixing bowl. Ad to butter mixture in several additions, mixing well after each addition. Stir dried cranberries & white chocolate chips. Drop by rounded teaspoonfuls onto ungreased cookie sheets. Bake for 10-12 minutes or until golden brown. Cool on wire cookie rack. Makes about 2-1/2 dozen cookies.

COMO DICE EL DICHO:

"COMERSE LA TORTA ANTES DEL RECREO"

Honky Tonk Girl Cake

Those of you who know me, and know me well, will know right away why I named this cake version Honky Tonk Girl. It is for my admiration as a true fan of the one and only Queen of Country, herself.

Ingredients:

2 cups sugar

3 whole eggs

½ tsp salt

1½ cups whole milk

2 tsp vanilla or almond extract

2/3 cup butter flavor shortening (I like to use CRISCO)

2¾ cups all-purpose flour

2½ tsp baking powder

Procedure:

Preheat oven to 350 degrees F, grease & flour two 9" round pans. Set aside. In a large bowl, cream butter shortening, sugar, eggs & extract, until fluffy. Add flour, baking powder, salt & milk. Beat on low speed until blended, scraping bowl occasionally. Pour into pans.

Bake at 350 degrees F for 35-45 minutes or until center springs back when it is lightly touched. Cool pans for 5 minutes. Remove & cool completely.

For icing:

1/3 cup butter flavored shortening

4 cups powdered sugar

2 tsp vanilla or almond extract

6-7 tsp milk

Procedure:

Combine powdered sugar, butter flavored shortening & extract. Slowly blend in milk to desired consistency. Beat on high for 5 minutes or until smooth & creamy. Frost sides & whole cake.

COMO DICE EL DICHO:

"COMES FRIJOLES Y ERUCTAS JAMON"

El Sabor De Mi Cocina

Momma's New York Cheesecake

While living in Michigan, my mother worked at a grocery store in the deli department. There she learned to bake special treats for the store's bakery. This was one of them and became a family must have for all occasions.

*Note: This recipe is only for half batch (1/2)

Ingredients:

3 pounds cream cheese

1½ cups sugar

3 whole eggs

3 tsp corn starch

1½ cups sour cram

1½ tsp vanilla

Procedure:

Mix cream cheese, sugar, eggs together until all blended. Next add corn starch, vanilla & sour cream & blend again, just enough to incorporate into mixture.

Pour into a greased round 10-12" cake pan (may require 2)

Bake in a pre-heated oven at 375 degrees F for 45 minutes to an hour. Or until toothpick inserted in center comes out clean & dry.

Top with your choice of berries.

For Chocolate Icing:

1 box powdered sugar

2 tbsp room temperature butter

Cocoa

Procedure:

Blend together until smooth adding a little more butter; a little at a time as needed to reach spreading consistency.

COMO DICE EL DICHO:

"COMIDA HECHA, AMISTAD DESHECHA"

Chocolate Mayonnaise Cake

Ingredients:

2 cups all-purpose flour

1 cup sugar

¼ cup baking cocoa

1 cup water

1 cup mayonnaise

1 tsp vanilla

Dash of salt

Powdered sugar

Procedure:

In a large mixing bowl, combine the dry ingredients. Add the water, mayonnaise & vanilla, beat on medium speed until well blended. Pour into a greased 9" square baking pan. Bake at 350 degrees F for 30 to 35 minutes or until a toothpick inserted near the center comes out clean. Cool on wire rack. Just before serving, sprinkle with powdered sugar.

COMO DICE EL DICHO:

"SOY COMO JUAN OROZCO – CUANDO COMO, NO CONOZCO"

Mexican Fruit Cake

A friend of mine in the state of Michigan passed on this recipe to me back in 2004. It does consist of fruits but not like our traditional FRUIT CAKE. It is a FRUIT CAKE, indeed.

Ingredients:

1 cup pecans
1 can crushed pineapple
2 cups sugar
1 tbsp baking soda
2 cups all-purpose flour
2 eggs well beaten

Procedure:

Mix all ingredients, pour into ungreased 9x13" pan and bake 30-40 minutes at 350 degrees F. or until toothpick inserted in center comes out clean.

Cream Cheese Icing:
Ingredients:
2 cups powdered sugar
8 oz cream cheese
1 stick butter
¼ tsp vanilla

Procedure:

Cream together butter & cheese, add sugar & vanilla. Spread over semi warm cake.

> COMO DICE EL DICHO: "COMIDA QUE MUCHO HIERVE, HASTA EL SABOR PIERDE"

Connie's Amish Way Funnel Cakes

While in the state of Michigan, living in the city of Hart, I had an Amish friend. She shared this Funnel Cake recipe with me. Ever since then, this is my favorite and the moistness in them are out of this world. I know you will love them.

Ingredients:

3 whole eggs, well beaten

2 cups whole milk

¼ cup sugar

4 cups all-purpose flour, sifted

2 tsp baking powder

½ tsp salt

Procedure:

Beat eggs as if for scrambling, to the beaten eggs add milk & sugar. In a separate bowl sift dry ingredients. Add to the egg mixture, beating until smooth. Heat oil to 375 degrees F & pour batter into hot fat through a regular household funnel.

Control the flow of the batter by holding your finger over the bottom of the funnel.

*When "cakes" are golden brown, drain & sprinkle with powdered sugar, serve warm.

COMO DICE EL DICHO:

"CUCHILLITO DE PALO, NO CORTA – PERO SI MAYUGA"

Corn Cake

This cake is done in the blender. It is my Pan de Elote but in the English version. Quite simple and quick for a Sunday luncheon dessert or just a plain ole anytime mid-day snack.

Ingredients:

3 whole eggs

3 – 4 fresh corn cobs (you can use 2 cans well drained corn in place of the fresh if you so desire)

1 stick of butter

1 can sweetened condensed milk

1 cup all-purpose flour – sifted

1 tbsp baking powder

2 tsp vanilla

½ cup whole milk

Procedure:

Pour all ingredients in blender as instructed above. Blend to a mix. Pour into a lightly greased & floured loaf pans & bake at 350 degrees F for about 30-40 minutes or until a toothpick inserted in the center of the cake comes out dry & clean.

COMO DICE EL DICHO:

"BOCA DE MIEL Y MANOS DE HIEL"

Dark as Mud Chocolate Cake

This cake is made using cocoa. I personally like to use Hershey's because the comparison between store brand and name brand, will just take it over the limit in the flavor.

Ingredients:

2 cups sugar
1¾ cups all-purpose flour
¾ cups Hershey's cocoa
1½ tsp baking powder
1½ tsp baking soda
1 tsp salt
2 whole eggs
1 cup whole milk
½ cup vegetable oil
2 tsp vanilla
1 cup boiling water

Procedure:

Heat oven to 350 degrees F & combine dry ingredients in a large bowl. Add eggs, milk, oil & vanilla. Beat for 2 minutes on medium speed. Stir in boiling water (note: batter will be very thin) & pour into two 9" round greased & floured pans. Bake 30-35 minutes, cool 10 minutes. Remove from pans to wire rack for complete cooling. Frost cake with following icing.

COMO DICE EL DICHO:

"COMO PEPITA EN COMAL CALIENTE"

El Sabor De Mi Cocina

Dark as Mud Chocolate Icing

Ingredients:

1 stick butter

2/3 cup Hershey's cocoa

3 cups powdered sugar

1/3 cup milk

1 tsp vanilla

Procedure:

Melt butter, stir in cocoa. Alternatively add powdered sugar & milk, beating on medium speed to spreading consistency. Add a little more milk if you need to. Add vanilla last and give it another quick mix, just enough to get the vanilla blended.

COMO DICE EL DICHO:

"COMO LA CHIA QUE NO ERA – PERO SE HACIA"

Marranito's - Piggy's

Molasses Cookies, these were my Grandpa Mache's all time favorite. Daddy loved them too, but if these were around, Grandpa would eat them all day long until the cookie jar emptied. I could still see him sitting at the end of the table with a cup of black coffee to wash them down.

Ingredients:

1¼ cup brown sugar
¼ cup vegetable shortening
1½ tsp baking soda
1½ tsp ground cinnamon
1 tsp ground ginger
1½ tsp vanilla
1 cup unsulphred molasses
1 whole egg
¼ cup milk
6 cups all-purpose flour

Egg wash: 1 whole egg

Procedure:

Preheat oven to 350 degrees F. in a large mixing bowl, stir together brown sugar, shortening, baking soda, cinnamon, ginger and vanilla until the mixture forms a firm paste. Add mixing after each addition, until well blended, the molasses, egg & milk. Gradually, add the flour, mixing to form a dough. Roll dough out to about ¼ inch thick; cut with a large pig shaped cookie cutter, place each Marranito on a cookie sheet lined with parchment paper. Or you can just place it on a pan with cooking spray.

For egg wash:

In a cup or a small bowl beat egg, using a pastry brush, paint tops of each Marranito lightly with beaten egg. Bake for 15-17 minutes or until browned.

COMO DICE EL DICHO:

"BOTELLITA DE JEREZ – TODO LO QUE ME DIGAS, SERA AL REVES"

Pastel de Tres Leches

While in high school, I met a great friend who is originally from Lampazos, Nuevo Leon – Mexico. And did I learn about so many different Mexican foods that we normally do not eat here. The first time she made this cake, I absolutely fell in love. The taste is so rich and feels so moist and creamy as you savor it in your mouth.

Recipe compliment of Marybel Mendoza – Jaime, Laredo, TX

Ingredients:

For the cake itself, I use my cake recipe either for Pan de 5 Tazas or the Snow-White Cake. (this is the only thing I changed out of this recipe. Everything else is authentic)

Make the cake according to its ingredients and procedures in this book.

Topping:

1 can sweetened condensed milk (14 oz)

1 can evaporated milk (12 oz)

1 cup heavy whipping cream

Whipped cream:

1 cup heavy whipping cream

3 tbsp powdered sugar

1 tsp vanilla

Procedure:

Preheat oven to 350 degrees F, grease a 13x9" baking pan and bake your cake according to recipe for either.

Cool this cake for 20 minutes once done.

Then, in a large bowl, whisk in topping ingredients until well blended. Use a skewer or fork to generously poke holes in, on top of semi warm cake. Pour milk mixture slowly over the cake, making sure all the poked holes are filled. Cool 30 minutes longer then refrigerate, covered for at least 4 hours or overnight.

For the topping, in a bowl, beat cream until it begins to thicken. Add powdered sugar & vanilla, beat until soft peaks start to form. Finally, spread over the entire cake and refrigerate at least another hour.

Cut and serve, topped with sliced strawberries, cherries, bananas, even peach slices will give this delicious cake an extra side kick.

COMO DICE EL DICHO:

"BUENO ES EL VINO - CUANDO ES FINO"

El Sabor De Mi Cocina

My Quick Peach Cobbler

Ingredients:

1 cup flour
1 cup sugar
2 tsp baking powder
1 stick margarine
3 cups peaches (usually about 5 large peaches)
¼ cup water
1 tsp vanilla
1 cup whole milk
Cinnamon & sugar to taste

Procedure:

Melt margarine & pour into a 9x13" pan.
Combine all dry ingredients in a separate bowl & mix.
Add 1 cup milk & 1 tsp vanilla to milk and mix well.
Pour that mixture in pan over the melted margarine or butter.
Place sliced peaches over the batter. Also, add the 1 cup of water over this batter & peaches.
Sprinkle with cinnamon & sugar to taste over the entire batter.

Bake at 375 degrees for 40 minutes.
Serve slightly warm with a scoop of vanilla ice cream.

COMO DICE EL DICHO:

"BUSCA Y HALLARAS - GUARDA Y TENDRAS"

Pan de Leche Condensada

(Sweetened Condensed Milk Cake)

Ingredients:

1 can 14 oz sweetened condensed milk
4 large whole eggs
1/3 cups butter
1 cup all-purpose flour
½ tsp baking powder
1 tsp vanilla

Procedure:

Preheat oven to 350 degrees F

Spray loaf pan with cooking spray

Pour milk in a mixing bowl, add eggs & mix with hand mixer just until well blended. Add butter & blend again. Next, blend in the baking powder & vanilla. Lastly, mix in the cup of all-purpose flour little at a time to avoid clumping.

Pour entire mixture into loaf pan & bake for about 40 minutes or until toothpick inserted in center comes out clean.

COMO DICE EL DICHO:

"CHIQUITO – PERO PICOSO"

Apple Crisp

Ingredients:

6 apples
2 tbsp granulated sugar
1¾ tsp ground cinnamon (divided – save some for a little later)
1½ tsp lemon juice
1 cup light brown sugar
¾ cup old fashioned oats
¾ cup all-purpose flour
½ cup cold unsalted butter, diced into small cubes

Procedure:

Preheat oven to 350 degrees F, butter an 8x8" baking dish. Or spray with non-stick cooking spray, set aside.

In a mixing bowl, add chopped apples, granulated sugar, ¾ tsp of the cinnamon & lemon juice. Stir to combine, then transfer to prepared baking dish.

In a separate mixing bowl, add topping ingredients; brown sugar, oats, flour, 1 tsp cinnamon and diced cold butter. Use a pastry cutter to cut the butter into the oat mixture, using a slight downward twisting motion, until the mixture resembles pea-sized crumbs.

Alternatively, you can use two forks or even your hands to cut the butter into the mixture.

El Sabor De Mi Cocina

Spread topping over the apples in the baking dish & gently pat to even it out. Bake 40-50 minutes until golden brown & bubbly.

Serve arm & enjoy...do not forget to add a scoop of vanilla ice cream if you want.

COMO DICE EL DICHO:

"NADIE SABE LO QUE TIENE – HASTA QUE LO VEN PERDIDO"

Empanaditas Borrachas

Ingredients:

Filling of your choice: Pineapple, pumpkin, etc.
7 cups all-purpose flour
2¼ cup vegetable shortening
½ cup sugar
2 tsp vanilla
Pinch of salt
1 can room temperature beer of your choice

Procedure:

Cream shortening, add flour, salt, sugar & mix slightly. Add the beer slowly. Continue to blend until all is incorporated. (do not knead the dough)

Start forming your little round balls of dough as if to make tortillas. You can roll them out like them too or just use a tortilla press.

Fill with about 1 to 2 tbsp of filling, depending on the size of the tortilla. Fold over, seal the edges with a fork & prick slightly the center of each to avoid explosion inside the oven. Bake 12-15 minutes at 450 degrees F. they will be light on top but golden brown on the bottom. Once done, take them from the oven, let them sit about 3-5 minutes then dust them in a mixture of cinnamon sugar or powdered sugar.

COMO DICE EL DICHO:

"CABALLO ALAZAN TOSTADO – ANTES MUERTO QUE CANSADO"

El Sabor De Mi Cocina

Chocolate Cherry "Dump It" Cake

Ingredients:

2 cans (21 oz each) cherry pie filling

1 box Betty Crocker super moist devil's food cake mix

¾ cup butter, melted

*Whipped topping or vanilla ice cream if desired

Procedure:

Heat oven to 350 degrees F, spray bottom of 13x9" glass baking dish with cooking spray.

Spread pie filling in baking dish. Top with dry cake mix, gently shake the pan to make sure batter is spread out evenly. Pour melted butter over the op with butter as possible.

Bake 42-45 minutes or until mostly dry on top & bubbly around the edges. Cool for 10 minutes before serving. Serve warm with whipped topping or ice cream as listed above.

COMO DICE EL DICHO:

"CABALLO, MUJER Y ESCOPETA - A NADIE SE LE PRESTAN"

El Sabor De Mi Cocina

Pumpkin Sugar Cookies

Ingredients:

½ cup softened butter

½ cup vegetable oil

½ cup pumpkin puree (canned pumpkin)

1 cup sugar

½ cup powdered sugar

½ tsp vanilla

2 large whole eggs

4 cups all-purpose flour

½ tsp baking soda

¼ tsp cream of tartar

½ tsp salt

1 tsp cinnamon

½ tsp nutmeg

For Glaze:

3 cups powdered sugar

4 tbsp water

1/3 tsp pumpkin pie spice (you can add less than the 1/3 - I do not like it too spicy)

Pinch of cloves for glaze

Procedure:

Preheat oven to 350 degrees F, line a baking sheet with parchment paper or a silicone baking mat & set aside. In a large bowl, stir butter, oil, pumpkin, sugars, vanilla & eggs together until incorporated & smooth. Slowly mix all dry ingredients until completely mixed. Scoop onto prepared baking sheet using 1 ½ tbsp scoop & flatten to ½" thick using the bottom of a glass. If the dough is sticking to the glass, press the bottom of the glass in regular sugar before flattening. Bake 8-9 minutes. While cookies bake, stir all ingredients together for the glaze until smooth.

Once cookies are finished baking, cool for 3 minutes on a baking sheet before transferring to cooling rack. Spread 1 ½ tsp of glaze over each warm cookie. Let glaze harden 2-3 hours before serving. Or eat them warm with lots of runny glaze.

COMO DICE EL DICHO:

"CARNE QUE SE LLEVA EL GATO –
NO VUELVE AL PLATO"

El Sabor De Mi Cocina

El Sabor De Mi Cocina

Beverages, Fudges, Candies, Salads, and More

Keto Drink

Ingredients:

1 sparkling Ice (16 oz)

   You can use any flavor

2 tbsp whipping cream

Procedure:

Get yourself an 8 oz glass, fill it ¾ full of ice (crushed or whole)

Pour in the sparkling water (making sure you do not over fill it)

Add 2 tbsp of whipping cream & stir

COMO DICE EL DICHO:

"COMO CAMOTE, Y QUE NO TE DE PENA - CUIDA TU CASA Y DEJA LA AJENA"

Chia Seed Pudding

Ingredients:

1 cup almond or whole milk

4 tbsp chia seeds

2 tbsp honey

½ tsp vanilla

½ tsp nutmeg

Procedure:

Blend all ingredients except chia seeds.

Stir in chia seeds & pour into a glass jar.

Refrigerate it for 4 hours to let it form a gel-like pudding texture.

Ready to eat!

COMO DICE EL DICHO:

"AVE QUE VUELA – A LA CAZUELA"

Pineapple Lemonade

Ingredients:

1 cup country time lemonade mix

3 cups cold water

1 can chilled pineapple juice (46 oz)

2 cans of sprite (12 oz each)

Procedure:

In a large pitcher, place water and add lemonade mix. Stir very well.

Add pineapple juice, stir again.

Now, add sprite, one can at a time and stir until completely mixed and the lemonade is dissolved.

Pour over ice – enjoy!

COMO DICE EL DICHO:

"Aserrin aserran, los maderos de San Juan, piden pan, y no les dan, piden queso, les dan hueso y les cortan el pescuezo!"

El Sabor De Mi Cocina

Agua de Horchata

(Rice Water)

Ingredients:

1 1/3 cup uncooked white long-grain rice
2 whole cinnamon sticks
4 cups water
1 cup milk (optional after milk cans are added)
2 tsp vanilla
1 (14) oz sweetened condensed milk
1 can evaporated milk
Ice

Procedure:

Soak rice & cinnamon sticks in 2 cups of hot water for 2 hours.

Combine the soaked rice mixture into the blender to blend until pasty & runny. Then use a small colander to get all the paste out & only use the liquid part of that, which is 2 cups. Add 2 tsp vanilla. Let sit for another 30 minutes in the mixture.

Add sweetened condensed milk, stir. Taste, this is where you add the cup of whole milk if desired. Only if you feel you want a creamier taste. Add remaining 2 cups of water and the ice to taste.

COMO DICE EL DICHO:

"HECHALE MAS CREMA A TUS TACOS"

Beef & Tomato Macaroni Soup

Ingredients:

2 tbsp vegetable oil

1 medium yellow onion, finely diced

1 green bell pepper, finely chopped

2 garlic cloves, minced

1-pound ground beef

2 tsp chili powder

2 tsp dried oregano

1 tsp salt

½ tsp black pepper

2 cans condensed tomato soup

1 (15 oz) can diced tomatoes, undrained

1 can 32 oz beef broth

4 cups water

2 cups elbow pasta, uncooked

Procedure:

Heat oil in a large pot, sauté onions, bell pepper & garlic until the vegetables begin to soften about 5-6 minutes.

Add the ground beef, breaking it up & cooking until there is no longer any pink. Drain off excess fat.

Stir in chili powder, oregano, salt & pepper.

Add condensed tomato soup, diced tomatoes with their juice, beef broth & water. Bring to a boil.

Once boiling, add the pasta, reduce the heat. Cover & simmer until the pasta is just tender. Adjust the seasoning and serve.

COMO DICE EL DICHO:

"BUENO, BONITO - Y BARATO"

El Sabor De Mi Cocina

Crockpot Lasagna Soup

Ingredients:
1-pound hamburger meat
½ onion, finely diced
1 whole red pepper, diced
1 (14.5 oz) diced tomatoes
1 (28 oz) can crushed tomatoes
1 tsp finely diced garlic
1 tbsp Italian seasoning
4 cups beef broth (1 carton)
12 oz lasagna noodles
1 cup mozzarella cheese
1 cup parmesan cheese
15 oz ricotta cheese

Procedure:

Brown hamburger meat.

Place meat in a 6-quart crockpot.

Add diced onions & red bell pepper.

Pour in the crushed tomatoes & diced tomatoes.

Add in the seasoning.

Pour in the beef broth.

Cover & cook on low for 5-6 hours.

Remove lid and break in the lasagna into bite size pieces and stir them in.

Cover & cook on high for about 30-40 minutes until noodles are soft.

Spoon into bowls, top with a tbsp of ricotta cheese if desired & a handful of mozzarella & parmesan cheese.

Enjoy with a side salad and garlic bread.

COMO DICE EL DICHO:

"AUNQUE SOMOS DEL MISMO BARRO – NO ES LO MISMO, CATRIN QUE CHARRO"

Slow Cooker Potato Soup

Ingredients:

5 large russet (or any kind) potatoes, peeled & diced

1 small onion, diced

4 cups chicken broth

3 tbsp butter

1 tsp minced garlic

1 tsp salt

1 tsp pepper

1 cup heavy cream

1/3 cup sour cream

1 tbsp corn starch

*Optional Toppings:

2 cups cheddar cheese

1 package of bacon, cooked & crumbled

Green onions, chopped up (as much as you want)

Procedure:

Add potatoes, diced onions, chicken broth, seasonings & butter to your slow cooker.

Cook on low 4-6 hours, or on high 3-4 hours until potatoes are soft.

About 30 minutes to an hour before it is done, in a small mixing bowl, whisk the heavy cream, sour cream & corn starch together. This will get thick.

Stir into the soup & cook on high for 20-30 minutes until the soup thickens slightly stirring occasionally.

Serve with your favorite toppings, such as cheddar cheese, sour cream, chives and/or bacon.

COMO DICE EL DICHO:

"BEBER Y COMER - SON COSAS QUE HAY QUE HACER"

Agua de Jamaica

(Hibiscus Water)

Ingredients:

2 quarts water

1 cup sugar to your desired taste

1 cup dried hibiscus flowers

½ cinnamon stick

Procedure:

In a large kettle, bring to boil water with sugar. Add cinnamon stick and boil until the sugar has dissolved.

Remove the kettle from the fire/heat, add the dried hibiscus flowers, cover and let sit for about 20 minutes.

Now, strain into a pitcher and throw out the seeped flowers and cinnamon stick.

(this is your concentrated Hibiscus for the water)

Add the remaining 4 cups of water to the concentrated and put in the refrigerator. If you would like the drink to be cold faster, then add ice cubes to your liking.

COMO DICE EL DICHO:

"HECHENSE UN TACO DE OJO"

Agua de Limon

(Limeade)

Ingredients:

4 large limes cut in fourths

6 cups of water

1 cup of sugar

Procedure:

Put half of the quartered limes in the blender with 1 cup of water.

Blend for about 5 seconds, strain on a mesh strainer into a pitcher.

Throw away the leftovers of the strained limes.

Put in the remaining half of the quartered limes in the blender once again with 1 cup of water.

Blend for another 5 seconds.

Strain the limes once more like in the beginning and throw away the leftovers. Add the sugar and remaining 4 cups of water to the pitcher and stir well. Add ice to a glass and serve to enjoy.

COMO DICE EL DICHO:

"DE MUSICO, POETA Y LOCOS - TODOS TENEMOS UN POCO"

Agua de Tamarindo

(Tamarind Water)

Ingredients:

15 tamarind pods

12 cups of water, divided

1 cup of sugar + more for taste

Procedure:

Peel the tamarind pods by removing and throwing away the hard shells that surround the pods. Also, throw away the strings inside the shell. They are not needed, only the pods.

Add 6 cups of water to your kettle and bring to boil on high heat. Add the peeled tamarind to the boiling water. Cover and bring the heat down to medium. Boil for an additional 8 minutes.

Remove kettle from heat, uncover and let it sit until it is completely cool. Usually a couple hours.

Using your hands, squeeze out the seeds from the tamarind pods. Discard, including the strings/fibers. Transfer the liquid and pulp to a blender and puree until smooth.

Pour the pureed liquid through a mesh strainer into a large pitcher. Use a spoon to stir the liquid in the strainer to help it make its way through. Throw away any pulp that does not go through.

Now, add the remining 6 cups of water and sugar to the pitcher. Stir it together to mix. Taste and sweeten to your liking. Add ice to an 8 oz glass and serve your tamarind water for a chilled flavor.

COMO DICE EL DICHO:

"EL AMOR DE LOS POBRES, ES COMO EL ESPINAZO DEL PUERCO - PELADO, PERO SABROSO"

Agua de Horchata con Fresa

(Strawberry Rice Water)

Ingredients:

1½ cups white rice, raw

7 cups water, divided

1 cinnamon stick

1-pound strawberries (could be fresh/frozen)

1 to 2 cups sugar (depending if you need to get it sweeter)

1 (14 oz) sweetened condensed milk (if you would rather sweeten with this instead of sugar)

1 can (14 oz) evaporated milk

Procedure:

In a large bowl, put the rice, 3 cups of water and cinnamon stick. Let sit in that water for at least 1 hour. But best left overnight to soften and absorb all the water to hydrate.

After the soaking is done, remove the cinnamon stick and add the rice along with the soaking water to a blender. Blend on high speed until mixture is completely mushed and smooth. Note: this may take a little longer due to the strength of the blender.

Next, using a mesh strainer, pour the rice water into a 2-quart pitcher. Throw away any left-over pulp that is left in the strainer.

Rinse the blender and add the strawberries, 1 cup sugar and the 4 cups water. Blend again until smooth. Using the strainer again, pour the strawberry puree into the rice water and stir. Add the milks at this point.

Taste to see if you need to add more sugar. But normally, the sweetened condensed milk is enough.

Pour into an ice filled glass and enjoy!

COMO DICE EL DICHO:

"DIOS NO ES VENGATIVO – PERO SI MUY JUSTICIERO"

Country Fudge

Ingredients:

½ can evaporated milk

2¼ cup sugar

¼ pound marshmallows

12 oz semi-sweet chocolate or white chocolate chips

1 cup nuts

1 tsp vanilla

Procedure:

In a pan on high heat, bring to a boil ½ can evaporated milk and 2 - ¼ cup sugar & vanilla.

Next turn down to medium heat, stirring constantly for about 10 minutes at its boil (as it is boiling)

Mix the marshmallows, chocolate chips & nuts. Have this ready. When the milk is already reached the 10 minutes boil, pour this mixture in with the milk & stir.

Pour all this in a spray greased 8x8" pan. Let cool down about 15-20 minutes before refrigerating to cool completely.

COMO DICE EL DICHO:

"EL QUE OBRA MAL – SE LE PUDRE EL TAMAL"

El Sabor De Mi Cocina

Corn Flake Candy

Ingredients:

1 cup karo syrup

1 cup sugar

1 tsp vanilla

1 cup peanut butter

6 cups corn flakes

Procedure:

Combine syrup, sugar & vanilla on low heat until it bubbles.

Then add peanut butter & mix well until peanut butter is melted. Remove from heat.

Add corn flakes one cup at a time & mix well. Put on wax paper or greased pan with a spoon. Let cool.

COMO DICE EL DICHO:

"AL QUE TODOS VAN A VER - CUANDO TIENEN QUE COMER - EL NOPAL"

El Sabor De Mi Cocina

Lake Effect Snow Almond Fudge

Ingredients:

¾ cup butter

3 cups sugar

2/3 cup evaporated milk

16 oz white chocolate bark

7 oz marshmallow cream

1 cup sliced almonds

½ tsp almond extract, to taste

½ cup sliced almonds, for topping

Procedure:

Grease 9x13" pan with softened butter. Break white chocolate into cubes & melt. In a 2 ½ - 3-quart saucepan combine first 3 ingredients, bring to a full boil over medium heat while stirring. Remove from heat, add white chocolate, stir well until smooth & well blended. Add almonds & almond extract.

Pour into pan, sprinkle sliced almonds on top. Cool, slice into squares then refrigerate.

COMO DICE EL DICHO:

"A GUSTO BEBERAS TU VINO – SIN MOLESTAR AL VECINO"

Maple Fudge

Note: You will need a candy thermometer for this recipe*

Ingredients:

2 cup maple syrup
1 tbsp light corn syrup
¾ cup half and half
1 tsp vanilla
¾ cup coarsely chopped walnuts

Procedure:

Combine maple syrup, corn syrup & half and half in a 1-1/2 quart saucepan. Place pan over moderate heat; stir constantly until mixture starts to boil. Continue cooking this mixture without stirring until it reaches 234 degrees F on the candy thermometer or until a small amount of syrup forms a soft ball in cold water.

Remove from heat, do not stir. Let mixture stand until it cools to lukewarm temperature about 110-120 degrees F.

Beat mixture until it thickens & begins to lose its gloss. Add vanilla & walnuts, pour immediately into a buttered 8x8x2" pan. When cool, cut into squares.

COMO DICE EL DICHO:

"MEJOR SOLA QUE MAL ACOMPAÑADA"

Church Windows

Ingredients:

1 (12) oz package chocolate or white chocolate chips

1 stick margarine

1 large bag colored miniature marshmallows

Wax paper

Procedure:

In a large saucepan on medium heat, slowly melt together the chocolate/ white chocolate chips and stick of margarine.

Remove from heat and add 1 large bag of colored marshmallows. Mix well and transfer to wax paper. Start forming into a roll (butter your hands to prevent burning since the mixture may be very hot).

Roll it up to cover with same wax paper, place on cookie sheet and refrigerate until cool enough to slice. About 2 hours. Slice accordingly - place in sandwich baggies to preserve.

COMO DICE EL DICHO:

"AHI QUE COMER, BEBER, BAILAR Y GOZAR - QUE EL MUNDO SE VA ACABAR"

Damiana's Fruit Salad

Recipe compliment, Cousin, Damiana Guerrero – Zapata, TX

1 can fruit cocktail, drained

1 can pineapple tidbits, drained

1 can cherry pie filling

1 can sweetened condensed milk

1 (8) oz tub cool whip

1 bag marshmallows (white)

Procedure:

Mix in all ingredients together in order – chill & enjoy. Just like that, simple as you read it.

COMO DICE EL DICHO:
"A LA HORA DE FREIR FRIJOLES – MANTECA ES LO QUE HACE FALTA"

Ramen Noodle Salad

Recipe compliment, Jean Ann Villarreal – Lone Rock, Iowa/Freer, TX

Ingredients:

1 small package coleslaw mix

½ cup matchstick carrots

1 package sunflower seed kernels

1 package chicken flavored Ramen noodle

1/3 cup vegetable oil

2 tbsp apple cider vinegar

¼ cup sugar

Packet chicken seasoning (included in Ramen package)

Dash of black pepper

Procedure:

In a large mixing bowl, add coleslaw, carrots, sunflower seed kernels & mix well.

Break apart the ramen noodles & add to coleslaw mix & stir well.

In a separate bowl, add oil, vinegar, sugar, seasoning packet & black pepper, mix well. Pour over the coleslaw mix and mix well. Stir before serving.

Note: The ramen in this salad gives it the perfect crunch. It will get soggy with the moisture. I like to add the noodles right before serving.

COMO DICE EL DICHO:

"HASTA A LA MEJOR COCINERA −
SE LE HUMEA LA OLLA"

Carne Seca

(Jerky)

Every year, during hunting season, my husband makes Deer Jerky. This is his way of preparing his batch.

Ingredients:

3 pounds meat (could be beef or whatever you want)

¾ cup Worcestershire sauce

2 tsp seasoned salt

2 tsp onion powder

1/3 cup soy sauce

2 tsp accent seasoning

1 tsp garlic powder

1 tsp ground black pepper

3 tbsp liquid hickory smoke

Procedure:

The best cut to use for deer is the legs, tenderloin/backstrap. If you have the whole ham chunks, slightly freeze before beginning to slice by hand. If using a slicer, completely freeze. This makes it easier on the slicer to get thin slices of meat.

Slice lengthwise ¼ - 3/8" thick, place thawed meat into a container & cover with ingredients listed above. Mix well. Marinate overnight in refrigerator. Next day, making sure it is not dripping, place in the dehydrator for 24 hours or hang to dry for several days until completely dehydrated.

For larger quantities, just volumize the recipe.

COMO DICE EL DICHO:

"ANDANDO A LA CARRETA - SE ACOMODAN LAS CALABAZAS"

El Sabor De Mi Cocina

Low Carb Cream Cheese Fudge

Ingredients:

1 stick salted butter

2 oz bakers unsweetened chocolate

1 tbsp vanilla

1 (8) oz package cream cheese softened

½ cup stevia or any sweetener of choice

Procedure:

Place butter & chocolate in a small pan & melt on low heat. When chocolate butter is just melted, add vanilla & sweetener then blend together. Place cream cheese in a medium bowl & pour chocolate mixture over it. With a hand mixer, mix about 2 minutes. Pour into a greased pan. Use a 6x8" pan & freeze it. Cut in squares. Makes about 18 – 24 pieces.

COMO DICE EL DICHO:

"A QUIEN LE DAN PAN – QUE LLORE"

Mango Ice Cream

This recipe calls for only 3 ingredients

Ingredients:

2 cups heavy cream
1 (14) oz sweetened condensed milk
2-3 large mangos
2 drops yellow food coloring, if desired to get a darker color of ice cream

Procedure:

Slice the mangos and scoop out the flesh, throwing out the seed and the skin. In a blender or food processor, add the mango and bring it to the consistency of applesauce.

In a large bowl, mix the mango pulp, condensed milk and heavy cream.

Use an electric mixer at low speed to beat the mixture until it begins to thicken. Bring the speed up to medium and continue to beat it for about 8-10 minutes or until you see stiff peaks start to form.

While beating, squeeze a few drops of the food coloring if you so desired to add it.

Pour the mixture into an 9x5" loaf pan & cover with seran wrap. Freeze for at least 6 hours or overnight. Serve it frozen.

COMO DICE EL DICHO:
"AQUI TE ESPERO – CON LA CUCHARA DEL PANADERO"

Peanut Butter Balls

Ingredients:

1 cup corn syrup

1 cup powdered sugar

1 cup peanut butter

1 tsp vanilla

3 cups rice krispies cereal

Procedure:

Stir together corn syrup & sugar in a large saucepan. Bring to a boil, stirring constantly.

Remove from heat & add peanut butter & vanilla.

Stir until smooth. Stir in cereal.

Drop by spoonful's on silicone mats or waxed paper. Cool slightly & roll into balls. Enjoy!

You can also roll in powdered sugar for a richer taste.

COMO DICE EL DICHO:

"A TODO PUERQUITO – SE LE LLEGA SU SAN MARTIN"

El Sabor De Mi Cocina

Quickie Fudge

Ingredients:

1 (14) oz can sweetened condensed milk

2 cups semi-sweet chocolate chips

Procedure:

Microwave the milk & chips for 1 minute. Stir until smooth – adding 15 seconds at a time back into the microwave until completely smooth.

Pour into an 8x8" pan lined with parchment paper. No need to spread it to the corners, this will spread itself and it will be thicker.

Let it set up, you can place it in the refrigerator.

Cut, eat & enjoy!

Note: You can substitute white almond bark for the chocolate chips.

COMO DICE EL DICHO:

"A QUIEN MADRUGA – DIOS LE AYUDA"

Homemade Queso Blanco

(White Mexican Cheese)

Ingredients:

1-gallon whole white milk or fresh from cow
1 junket rennet tablet
1 thermometer
1 large kettle

Procedure:
In a large kettle, put in the gallon of milk. Take to the stove on med/high heat stirring consistently until the milk is about 70-75 degrees F on thermometer, remove from heat.

Use 1 junket rennet tablet, hammer it in the package until it is powder.

Put it in about ¾ cup of the warm milk & mix it good. Put it back into the large kettle with the milk at room temperature by now, until you start to see it curd.

Set the kettle on the fire again until the whey is separated from the milk.

Press the curd on a cheese cloth to remove the excess whey. Put the cheese on a pan so that most of the whey is gone and the cheese can be handled. Then let it dry some more.

COMO DICE EL DICHO:

"AGUA DE LAS DULCES MATAS, TU ME CUIDAS, TU ME MATAS - TU ME HACES ANDAR A GATAS"

El Sabor De Mi Cocina

Connie's "Munkey" Caviar Dip

Ingredients:

1 large bag Fritos brand scoops

2 cans Mexicorn – corn (or regular corn)

1 can rotel (mild or hot)

2 cups shredded cheddar cheese (I like to use the Colby Jack)

6 green onions (sliced)

1 cup Real Mayonnaise

1 cup sour cream

Procedure:

Mix all together except the corn chips. 😊 Ha Ha Ha, they are used to scoop the dip & eat it. Make sure to drain the corn. You will love this.

*Sorry friends & family, there is no REAL caviar in this dip

COMO DICE EL DICHO:

"AHORA ES CUANDO, CHILE VERDE – LE HAS DE DAR SABOR AL CALDO"

Pumpkin Spice Cream Cheese Spread

Ingredients:

½ cup plain pumpkin puree

8 oz cream cheese softened

¼ cup regular sugar

½ tsp vanilla

¼ tsp ground cinnamon

1/8 tsp nutmeg

Procedure:

In a large bowl with a hand mixer, whip pumpkin & softened cream cheese together until color changes a little.

Scrape the edges & mix on low, sprinkling sugar into the mixture once the sugar is mixed in, stir in the remaining ingredients. Scrape the edges & whip again to ensure a completely smooth mixture.

Spoon into a small bowl, cover with seran wrap & refrigerate until ready to use.

This is great on bagels or English muffins.

COMO DICE EL DICHO:

"ALGO TIENE EL AGUA - CUANDO LA BENDICEN"

Gooey Popcorn Balls

Ingredients:

1 cup butter

1 cup light corn syrup

2 cups packed light brown sugar

½ cup regular sugar

14 oz sweetened condensed milk

1 tbsp vanilla

15 - 30 cups popped popcorn - keep in mind that less popcorn will be messier and gooier

Procedure:

Bring butter, syrup & sugars to a boil. Keep bubbling over medium heat until it hits the softball stage, 240 degrees, using a candy thermometer.

Add sweetened condensed milk, vanilla & boil 1 more minute. Let cool a few minutes so it does not shrink the popcorn & stir.

For gooey caramel popcorn:

Use 2-3 batches of air popped popcorn for this, serve immediately.

For popcorn balls:

Use 1 - 1 ½ batches of air popped popcorn for these balls.

Spread the popcorn out & let it start to cool. Spray your hands with cooking spray & portion it out into 8 sections and ball it up.

Continue to check back & ball, turn until they cool enough that they stay in their ball shape.

COMO DICE EL DICHO:

"AL NOPAL LO VAN A VER - SOLO CUANDO TIENE TUNAS"

My Grandmother's Dulce de Leche

aka Leche Quemada (Mexican Milk Fudge)

I remember my Grandmother, she loved to make this Mexican Fudge, Leche Quemada as we traditionally say today. She would stand by the stove for a couple hours or so to make this delicious candy. Then, in the blink of an eye, all gone. That, is, how good it is.

Ingredients:

2 - 12 oz cans evaporated milk
    (Nestle Carnation or Pet Evaporated milk is recommended)
5½ cups sugar
5½ tbsp butter, not margarine
1 tsp salt
½ cup brown sugar

Procedure:

Mix milk, sugar, butter & salt in a large heavy pan & bring to a boil on medium to high heat.

Add brown sugar & stir until it dissolves. Continue cooking & stirring the mixture over the medium heat until it reaches softball stage, 240 degrees on candy thermometer.

Stir until thick enough, as for fudge. Drop by teaspoonfuls on a buttered pan or waxed paper. Or pour onto a buttered pan & cut into squares.

COMO DICE EL DICHO:
"AL OJO DEL AMO - ENGORDA EL CABALLO"

Atole de Avena

(Oatmeal)

Ingredients:

1 cup old fashioned oats

3 cups water

1 cinnamon stick

1 cup brown sugar

2 cups whole milk

2 cups evaporated milk

2 tbsp salted butter

1 tsp vanilla

Procedure:

Ina large pot bring the water & cinnamon stick to a boil.

Once boiling add the oats & reduce the heat to low. Simmer for 25 minutes, stirring occasionally to prevent sticking.

Add the sugar & stir well. Then add the milk, vanilla & the butter, stir again.

Continue to simmer for about 15 minutes or until the Atole is nice and hot. Serve and add more milk if desired.

COMO DICE EL DICHO:

"A CADA UNO LE TOCA ESCOGER - LA CUCHARA CON LA QUE HA DE COMER"

Champurrado

Ingredients:

1½ cups water
1 cinnamon stick
1 whole clove
1-star anise
4½ cups milk
2 tablets Mexican chocolate
  (Ibarra or Abuelita)
¾ cup pinole
  (ground corn flour – such as maseca)
1 pinch crushed piloncillo
  (Mexican brown sugar cone) you can add
    More to your taste.

Procedure:

Bring water, cinnamon stick, clove and star anise to a boil in a saucepan, remove from heat and allow spices to steep until water is releasing the smell of the spices added.

Usually about 10 minutes. When done strain to keep just the water.

Heat milk, chocolate and corn flour in another saucepan over medium heat, whisking until chocolate is dissolved and the liquid is thickened, about 10 minutes. Remove from heat and add piloncillo, let rest until sugar is dissolved, about 5 more minutes. Pour cinnamon water into chocolate mixture and stir to combine.

COMO DICE EL DICHO:

"AL QUE LE PIQUE – QUE SE RASQUE"

Potato Candy

Ingredients:

½ cup mashed potatoes – about 2 large
½ cup, (1 stick) salted butter, softened
6-7 cups powdered sugar plus additional for dusting
2 tsp vanilla
Creamy peanut butter for filling

Procedure:

Combine mashed potatoes, butter and one cup of sugar in a large bowl & use an electric mixer to combine.

Add remaining sugar, 1 cup at a time & stir until mixed after each addition. Once you have added 6 cups of powdered sugar, check the consistency. If the dough is not moldable in your hands and can not be rolled into a ball, then, continue to add sugar until it is firm.

Stir in vanilla.

Refrigerate for at least 1 hour. If you chill longer it may become too firm and brittle and will just need to sit at room temperature for 10 - 15 minutes until it is workable.

Once chilled, divide the dough into 2 pieces & place one piece on a clean surface so that you have generously dusted it with powdered sugar. Dust the surface of the dough with additional sugar. Use a rolling pin to roll the dough out into a large rectangle about ¼ "thick. If your dough is too sticky or falls apart, you will need to add more sugar. Reshape it into a ball and start over.

Once the dough has been rolled into a ¼" thick rectangle, spread evenly with peanut butter, leaving a small amount of space peanut butter free around the perimeter of the dough.

Starting with the longer side of your rectangle, gently but tightly roll into a log.

Use a knife to slice into pieces about ¼ - ½ "thick.

Repeat steps with remaining half of dough.

Serve & enjoy - store left over candy in an airtight container in the refrigerator for up to a week.

COMO DICE EL DICHO:
"AL OJO DEL AMO - ENGORDA EL CABALLO"

Atole de Arroz

(Rice Pudding)

1 ½ cups long-grain white rice, uncooked
2 cups water
1 large cinnamon stick or 2 small ones
3 cups whole milk
1 cup evaporated milk
½ can sweetened condensed milk
1 tsp vanilla (if you want a non-yellowish color use clear vanilla)
2 tbsp salted butter
1/3 cup raisins
Sugar to taste if needed (condensed milk is already sweet)

El Sabor De Mi Cocina

Procedure:

In a large saucepan or pot, combine water, rice and cinnamon sticks, bring to a boil. Reduce heat & simmer. Add raisins & cover pot to heat for 10 minutes or until the water is absorbed.

Add the milks, cover and continue to cook over a low heat for another 15-20 minutes, stirring after 8-10. The mixture will thicken as the rice absorbs the milk. At this point, I add the 2 tbsp of butter & vanilla. This gives my Atole a sweet, yet salty flavor. Continue to simmer, uncovered for 3-5 minutes.

Once thickened enough to your liking, it is now done. Serve and sprinkle with ground cinnamon for the extra garnish kick if desired. You can serve this hot or cold.

COMO DICE EL DICHO:

"A BUEN SANTO - TE ENCOMIENDAS"

Atole de Pinole

Ingredients:

½ cup cornmeal

2 cups water

1 cinnamon stick, broken up into 3 pieces

32 oz milk

½ cup sugar

1 tsp vanilla

Procedure:

In a skillet, bring the ½ cup cornmeal & toast it, stirring it consistently to avoid the cornmeal to burn. You want it to be golden brown. While that is going on, bring to boil in a large pot/kettle the 2 cups of water, vanilla & the broken cinnamon stick, on medium heat for 5 minutes.

Once the water is boiling, with a whisk stir the water, as you slowly add the toasted cornmeal. When it is all incorporated, add the milk and sugar, let cook down for another 10 minutes, stirring to prevent sticking at the bottom of the kettle. Serve warm in cups, drink up and enjoy.

COMO DICE EL DICHO:

"ACABANDOSE EL DINERO – SE TERMINA LA AMISTAD"

El Sabor De Mi Cocina

Lemon Pepper Marinade

Ingredients:

1/3 cup lemon juice

¼ cup vegetable oil

½ tsp black pepper

2 tbsp water

2 tsp fresh or dried dill leaves, chopped

1 tsp salt

1 garlic clove, sliced and minced

Procedure:

In a medium to large bowl, add the lemon juice, and slowly whisk in the oil until mixed. Add the remaining ingredients and continue to whisk it for a few seconds.

Let the mixture stand for at least 10 minutes before using it to marinate a chicken or turkey. (if you plan to use this marinate for your turkey, then double up on the recipe)

Tip Hint: A chicken marinated for 2 hours, a turkey for 4.

COMO DICE EL DICHO:

"EL GALLO SERA MUY GALLO – PERO LA DE LOS HUEVOS ES LA GAILLINA"

El Sabor De Mi Cocina

Grilled Turkey Marinate

This is the perfect marinate if you plan to grill the turkey for your Thanksgiving dinner.

Ingredients:

1½ cups light cooking vegetable oil

½ cup water

½ cup lemon juice

½ cup white vinegar

½ cup Worcestershire sauce

¼ cup balsamic vinegar

1 tbsp dried oregano

1 tbsp salt

1 tbsp ground black pepper

Procedure:

Combine all the ingredients listed above very well.

Keep refrigerated until you need to use it and mix before adding it to the turkey.

COMO DICE EL DICHO:
"DE MUSICO, POETA Y LOCO – TODOS TENEMOS UN POCO"

Connie's Pea Salad

Even if you do not like peas, this you will like. There is more to it than just peas.

Ingredients:

2 cans peas, well drained and rinsed

¼ cup Real Mayonnaise (add more or less on how creamy you like it)

2 hard boiled eggs, cooled, peeled and diced

4 tbsp real bacon bits (add more or less to your desired preference)

½ onion, semi finely diced

4 tbsp dill pickle relish

4 tbsp finely diced celery (if desired)

Procedure:

Mix all the above listed ingredients in a medium bowl. Adding the mayonnaise last. Chill in the refrigerator and serve with ritz crackers or as a side for any dish.

COMO DICE EL DICHO:

"DEJAR DE COMER POR HABER COMIDO – NO HAY NADA PERDIDO"

Terry and Ruthann's Campfire Delight

While living in the state of Michigan, I met a wonderful couple, that always went over and beyond to help us in any which way or form.

At the time we were living at a campground by Hart Lake in Hart, Michigan. There, in the evenings a lot of the camping people would gather around an outside campfire. And my friend Ruthann would make these delicious campfire delights. Usually we could feel the chill of an early fall while we surrounded the campfire.

Ingredients:

2 slices white bread

Margarine

1 tsp chocolate chips

1 tsp peanut butter chips

1 tsp crushed pecans

½ tsp flaked coconut

1 campfire bread cast iron roaster

Or you can do them on the stove inside anytime.

Procedure:

Coat one side of each of the bread slices with margarine.

Place the side with the margarine onto each of the sides of the cast iron roaster. Then while the side with no margarine is facing you, start adding the chips, pecans, coconut flakes and top with the other slice of bread that has no margarine on top of the chips layered on the previous slice. Top it with the 2nd half of the cast iron roaster and bring to the fire to roast/toast. Flipping the roaster from one side to the other, making sure both sides have toasted the bread evenly. Usually about 5 minutes. If you notice that it needs more toasting, just take it back to the fire a little longer. Remove from the fire being cautious for this is extremely hot, the chips have now melted and can cause serious burns.

Note: if you will do this indoors, it is basically the same procedure just that you will be making them as if you were making a grilled cheese sandwich.

COMO DICE EL DICHO:

"DE TAL PALO – TAL ASTILLA"

Debbie's Apple Dip

Up north, in the state of Michigan, where I lived for 15 years, not only do you see all 4 seasons at its finest. We also see the many harvest seasons, such as cherry, peach, asparagus, pickle, squash, corn and apple. Thus, the apple season, is where this favorite comes to play. One of my best friends up there, would always make this to share with her group of co-workers. Including me, for at the time, we worked night shift at the City of Hart's local nursing home.

Ingredients:

1 (8oz) package cream cheese

Brown sugar to taste

1 tsp vanilla

Apples - skinned, cored and sliced

Procedure:

In a medium bowl bring the cream cheese and whip it on low speed with an electric mixer until smooth.

Add brown sugar to taste and mix with a fork to blend it into the cheese.

For the extra added flavor, add 1 tsp vanilla. Blend and enjoy with sliced apples.

COMO DICE EL DICHO:
"DE LENGUA - ME COMO UN PLATO"

Agua de Sandia

(Watermelon Water)

Ingredients:

3 cups peeled and seeded watermelon, cubed

½ cup sugar or more if needed to your taste

4 cups water for puree

6 cups water for actual agua/water

Procedure:

Puree the cubed watermelon with 4 cups of water in a blender until smooth. Pour into a pitcher. Add 6 cups of water to the pitcher with the watermelon puree and stir. Sweeten with the required sugar to taste. Serve over an ice filled glass and enjoy.

COMO DICE EL DICHO:

"DETRAS DE UN GRAN HOMBRE – HAY UNA GRAN MUJER"

El Sabor De Mi Cocina

Semita de Marybel

This recipe comes from somewhere in Nuevo Leon, Mexico. It was shared to me by one of my best friends from high school.

Ingredients:

4 cups flour

5 tbsp lard

1 piloncillo cone, shredded

¼ tsp salt

1 tsp baking powder

15 anise stars

½ cup raisins

½ cup pecans

Procedure:

Boil star anise in 1 cup of water for 5 minutes.

Blend flour, salt, baking powder and mix lightly. Add lard. But do not overmix.

To that, add shredded piloncillo, raisins, mix gently. Add ½ cup star anise tea and blend slightly with out overworking the dough.

Let it rest 10 minutes. Cut in ½ and roll out about ½ to 1" thick on floured surface.

Add pecan ½'s all around and in center. Bake for 15 minutes on a cookie sheet at 350 degrees F or until lightly golden brown.

Tip: As soon as it is out of the oven, I like to brush it with lots of butter and then sprinkle in more shredded piloncillo or even dark brown sugar all over.

COMO DICE EL DICHO:

"DIOS NO CUMPLE ANTOJOS – NI ENDEREZA JOROBADOS"

El Sabor De Mi Cocina

Christmas Day Jam

Ingredients:

2 packages frozen whole strawberries

1 pound fresh or frozen cranberries

5 pounds sugar – (yes, you heard it correctly)

2 pouches liquid fruit pectin (3 oz each packet)

Procedure:

In a large food processor, bring together the strawberries and the cranberries. They can be processed to a puree texture for a smooth jam. Or you can leave some chunks to have it chunkier.

Pour the pureed fruit into a large kettle. Add sugar over medium high heat. Bring it together to a rolling boil for 1 minute once it starts to boil.

Remove the kettle from the heat and add the pectin, stirring quickly to mix completely.

Then, allow the jam to cool for 5 minutes and remove the foam that forms atop.

Now, you can add your hot jam mixture into sterile ½ pint jars, leaving ¼" headspace. Wipe away any excess fruit around the rims with a clean cloth. Cover with the hot lids and place on the jar heads.

Bring them ½ pint jars to a water bath for 10 minutes.

This will usually give you around 12-14 jars.

COMO DICE EL DICHO:

"DANDO Y DANDO – PAJARITO VOLANDO"

Pico de Gallo

Ingredients:

1 cup finely chopped white onion

1 medium jalapeno or serrano pepper (remove the seeds if you want a milder mix)

¼ cup lime juice

¾ tsp salt – to taste

1½ pounds ripe red tomatoes (about 8 Roma or 4 large), diced

½ cup finely chopped cilantro (1 bunch)

Procedure:

In a medium bowl, bring together the onion, jalapeño, lime juice and salt. Let it sit for about 5 minutes while you dice the tomatoes and cilantro.

Add the tomatoes and cilantro to the bowl and stir to combine. Taste, and add more salt if you think it needs more.

Let entire mixture sit for 15 minutes or a few hours in the refrigerator before serving. Keep covered for a longer last.

COMO DICE EL DICHO:

"AQUI ME DIERON GATO – POR LIEBRE"

Salsa Verde

Ingredients:

1½ pound tomatillos or green tomatoes
1 onion
4 serrano chiles
4 cloves garlic
12 sprigs of fresh cilantro
2 tbsp cooking oil
1½ tsp salt to taste

Procedure:

If using the tomatillos, remove the papery husks from them and rinse them to remove the tackiness they carry.

Cut the onion in chunks. Add all the ingredients except the cilantro and salt, to a large pot and cover all the ingredients with water.

Bring the water and the ingredients to a boil and let them simmer for 10 minutes.

Blend all the boiled ingredients in a blender with the cilantro, adding just a little boiled broth as needed to get the consistency of your Salsa Verde. (You do not want it too thick nor too runny.)

Now, heat the 2 tbsp of cooking oil in a skillet and pour in the blended salsa into the oil. You will hear the sizzling as you pour it. Bring down the heat and let simmer for 20 minutes.

COMO DICE EL DICHO:

"DE AMOR CALDO - Y DE CARIDAD FRIJOLES"

Salsa Roja

Ingredients:

5 Roma tomatoes

1 onion

12 sprigs of fresh cilantro

2 serrano chiles

2 cloves of garlic

1 tsp salt to taste

2 tbsp cooking oil

4 cups water

Procedure:

Bring together a medium bowl for all the ingredients listed above.

Cut onion in chunks and tomatoes in half. Cut off the stems from the serranos, slice them in half and remove the seeds if you want a milder salsa.

Peel the garlic clove and add all the ingredients to the kettle except the cilantro and salt.

Add enough water to almost cover the ingredients, only about 4 cups of water.

Bring that to a boil and reduce to low. Simmer for 20 minutes.

Blend all the ingredients including the cilantro with the cooking water. You can blend it in the blender in 2 batches so that it is well combined.

Heat 2 tbsp cooking oil in a separate skillet over medium heat. Pour in the blended salsa into the hot oil. You will hear it sizzle as you pour, pouring slowly to prevent being burned. Bring down to low, enough to heat and simmer the salsa. Let cool completely when done after 10 minutes of cooking in oil.

COMO DICE EL DICHO:

"CUANDO DOS SE QUIEREN BIEN – CON UNO QUE COMA BASTA"

Empanadas de Esmeralda

(Pumpkin Filled)

This dough can be used for filling of any kind. Here my Mom chose to use the traditional relleno de calabaza.

Ingredients for Dough:

3 cups all-purpose flour
¼ to ½ tsp salt
6 oz butter (1 stick and additional 4 oz) softened to room temperature
Milk or water – as needed to knead the dough
2 eggs
1 cup sugar
1 tsp anise seed

Procedure:

In a large mixing bowl, add flour, salt, sugar, anise seed and mix to blend all dry ingredients.

Now add the butter and eggs to incorporate into the flour mixture. Next, add milk or water as needed to knead the dough but not too much as you want it to resemble dough for tortillas. If the dough ends up too sticky, let sit for ½ an hour to absorb the extra fluid in it.

Now start forming the small balls to create the shapes of the rounds for the filling of the empanadas. Again, as if making tortillas.

Pumpkin Filling:

1 medium Halloween pumpkin
¼ cup anise seed
6 cups sugar (more if needed to taste)
1 tbsp all spice
3 cups brown sugar or 2 piloncillo cones
4 tsp vanilla
1 stick butter

Procedure:

Wash and cut the pumpkin, take out all the seed and strings from inside.

Cut pumpkin into pieces and bring to boil until tender.

Take skin off when cooked and cool. Spoon into a deep kettle and let cook while mashing down with a bean masher.

Now add in all the above listed ingredients and cook down on low to medium heat, stirring consistently until pumpkin puree gets to thickened stage. (not watery)

If at any point it seems to be too watery, simply add some corn starch for thickening.

Now the filling is ready to fill the dough rounds.

Fill about 2 tbsp in the center of each round and fold over. Seal around the edges with a fork to imprint the seal. This helps the empanada to prevent leakage of filling.

Do Not add any Water!

COMO DICE EL DICHO:

"CUANDO NO LLUEVE – TRUENA"

El Sabor De Mi Cocina

Tejano Coleslaw

Ingredients:

1 (14 oz) bag coleslaw mix

½ cup red bell pepper diced

½ cup black beans, rinsed & drained

½ cup whole kernel corn, rinsed & drained

½ cup finely chopped cilantro

1 jalapeno finely diced, seeded

¾ cup Real Mayonnaise

¼ cup sour cream

½ package taco seasoning, your choice brand

2 tbsp lemon juice

Procedure:

In a large bowl, bring to mix the coleslaw, red bell pepper, beans, corn, cilantro and jalapeno.

In another bowl, combine the mayo, sour cream, taco seasoning and lemon juice.

Add this mixture to the already mixed coleslaw and stir to combine.

Chill before serving.

COMO DICE EL DICHO:

"BIEN SABE EL FRIO - DONDE SE ARRIMA"